Day Trading for Beginners

Make Winning Trades Using Simple and Proven Trading Strategies in the Financial Markets Today with Zero Trading Experience Required

A.Z Penn

TABLE OF CONTENTS

HOW TO GET THE MOST OUT OF THIS BOOK

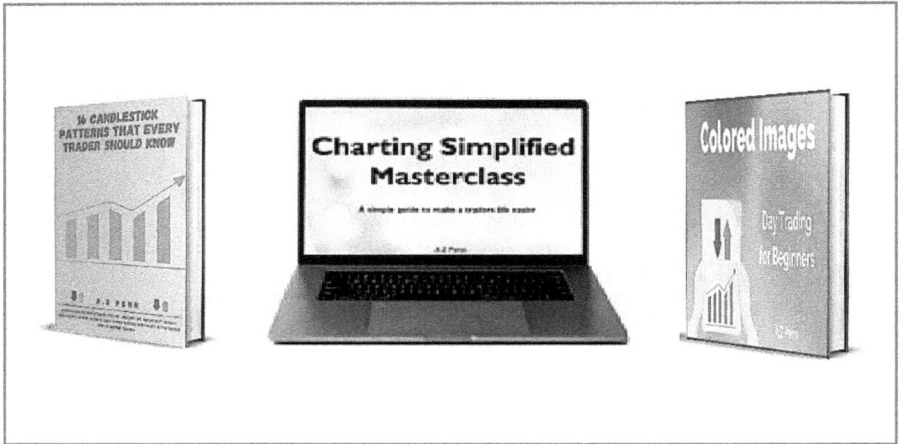

To help you along your trading journey, I've created a free bonus companion masterclass which includes video analysis of real life stock examples to expand on some of the key topics discussed in this book. I also provide additional resources that will help you get the best possible result.

I highly recommend you sign up now to get the most out of this book. You can do that by going to the link or scanning the QR code below:

www.az-penn.com

Free bonus #1: Charting Simplified Masterclass ($67 value)

In this 5 part video masterclass you'll be discovering various simple and easy to use strategies on making profitable trades. By showing you real life stock examples of a few charting indicators - you will be able to determine whether a stock is worth trading or not.

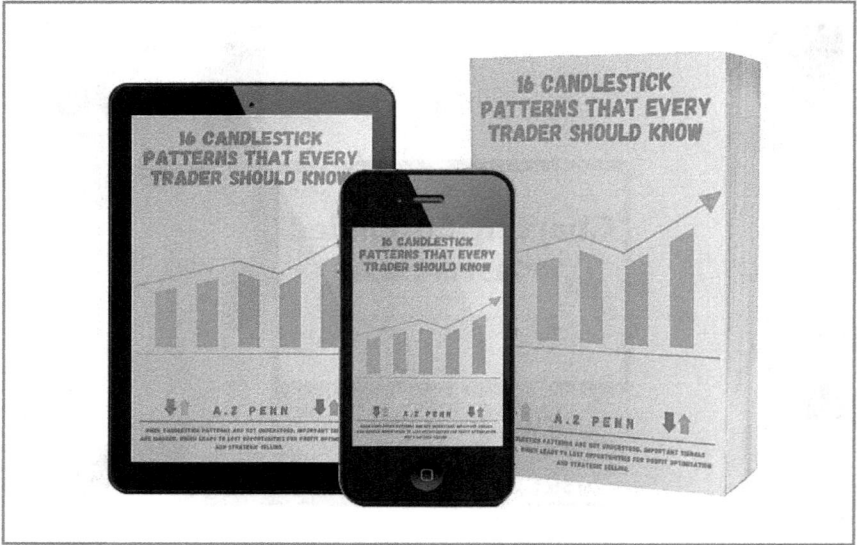

Free bonus #2: 16 Candlestick Patterns that Every Trader Should Know ($17 value)

Stay ahead in the trading game with our essential guide on the patterns that are vital for reading market signals, identifying trend reversals, and making profitable trades. Equip yourself with the knowledge to make informed decisions and maximize your trading returns.

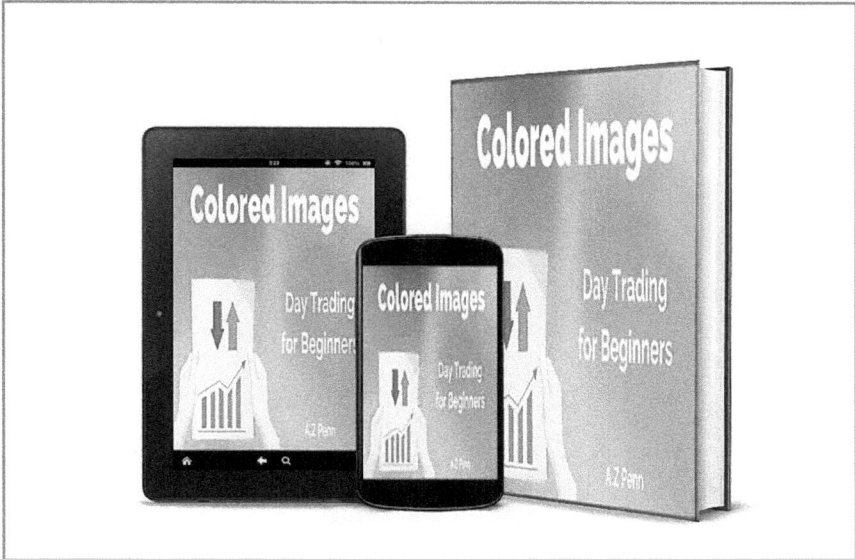

Free bonus #3: Colored Images – Day Trading for Beginners

To keep our books at a reasonable price for you, we print in black & white. But here are all the images in full color.

All of these bonuses are 100% free, with no strings attached. You don't need to provide any personal details except your email address.

To get your bonuses, go to the link or QR code:

www.az-penn.com

Introduction

Let's give you the bad news first. The shocking fact is that 80% of rookie day traders quit within their first two years. 40% don't even make it to the end of their first quarter. If you're going to succeed in day trading, you're going to need to be an exception to the rule.

Even experienced day traders can sometimes go wrong. At first, you might be a success like Matthew Jay, who had six successful years making good money. But he wanted more - more money, more risk, more excitement. He started making bigger and bigger trades. Eventually, he lost $127,000 before he managed to regain control. You can watch his video on YouTube by searching "How I Lost 127k Day Trading the Stock Market!!"

Day trading is tough and I'm going to show you things the way they are, with no sugar coating. Day trading is not a get rich quick scheme. You might as well say that starting a search engine or making electric cars is a get rich quick scheme. Yes, it worked for Google, and it worked for Tesla... but day trading is hard work if you want to get it right.

Why do so many day traders quit so quickly? Some expected a lot more profit much more quickly, and just ran out of enthusiasm. Some are scared by a run of losing trades. Some are bored; they thought day trading would be fun, but it turns out watching stocks move isn't the most fascinating way for spending a day. Some just lack confidence, and of course, some never really get started, often because they can't see where they need to focus their efforts.

Often, too, they jump into the market without being adequately prepared. They haven't read enough about trading, they haven't set their trading station up properly, they haven't backtested their strategy or 'paper traded' for long enough to sharpen their reactions. So they make easy mistakes, get panicked, have a series of losing trades, and decide trading is too hard for them to hack.

Have you done a few trades and had a poor experience? Or do you want to day trade but you're not quite sure how to get started? There's so much information out there on the internet these days from YouTube content creators and brokerage firms and trading systems, but it's often contradictory and you never know whether you can trust it. If these are your issues, I think this book will help.

Yes, this book will teach you how to read charts, identify potentially profitable situations, and trade them. But more importantly, this book will teach you how to manage your trades as a business; how to identify and focus on the best situations instead of having a scatter-gun approach to the markets; how to manage your risk so that you never bet the bank, and come out ahead more of the time; and how to find the right strategies, which are those that will be most effective for you - not necessarily the same ones that work for me.

In between, you'll learn how markets work, how to choose what assets to trade - though we'll concentrate mainly on stocks - and how to deal with a losing trade (because make no mistake, it will happen).

This book *won't* teach you exactly how to do any particular trade. You will need to develop your own trading system - that's part of the job, and you'll need to refine it as you continue to trade. Imagine you are a chef, you might start off with some very basic recipes, but you'd soon want to develop your own twist on the old favorites or develop your own signature dish. Trading is the same; you can start with tried and tested strategies, but over time, you'll find your favorites, and you'll find little extra touches that will boost your profitability.

To succeed as a day trader, you only need to find three or four types of situations that make you money. You don't need to be able to read every kind of chart and trade every market. When you start, it may take you a while to find out what are the trades that really 'click' for you. Maybe you should try a few different setups while you're still a junior trader. But when you focus on the trading strategies that work best for you, you'll be doing less work for better results, and you can vastly increase your profitability.

So, in this book, I'm not selling my system of trading. I do trade, and I make money at it, though it's not my full-time job. I also invest for the long term, so I know just how different the worlds of the day trader and the investor are; I have to 'change hats' several times a day!

Both as an investor and as a trader, I've made plenty of mistakes on my way to becoming more successful, but I've learned from them. I've also read a lot of different trading books, some of which were really thought-provoking and useful, and others less so. In this book I try to boil down everything I've learned to the essentials, and give you what you need to know to get started. I'll talk you through all the different types of trades you might consider, but most importantly, I'll give you a way to structure your trading business so that you find your optimum style and get the best returns you can.

So, shall we begin?

1

Chapter 1: Is Day Trading Right For You?

The first step on the way to becoming a successful day trader is to understand what exactly day trading involves, and assess whether it's a lifestyle that is going to suit you. Along the way, we might need to address a few myths about day trading - there are quite a lot of those! So, let's look at what day trading actually is, first of all.

What is day trading?

The first thing to understand is that day trading is not the same as investing. In fact, although traders and investors use the same markets, the two ways of making money are as different as night and day. An investor generally looks at buying a financial asset over the medium to long term. They may be interested in getting income from that asset, for instance dividends from a company, or interest payments from a Treasury bond. Investors need to think about the quality of what they're buying; they ask questions like "Is this a good company?" or "Is Germany likely to default on its bonds?"

A trader, on the other hand, is simply aiming to buy an asset now and sell it at a profit. If a trader sees a chance to trade a company that's really on its beam ends, has a lousy product and terrible financials, they will - unless it's likely to go bankrupt in the immediate future. The question is, will it go up? And if there's a good reason that it should, they'll buy it.

As a trader, you don't care about the long-term future of IBM, or the German economy, or what is going to happen to the world shipping markets. You are simply a speculator; you care exclusively about making a profit out of each of your trades.

Day trading is a particular subset of trading, in which you close out all your positions at the end of the day. You do not have any trading positions open overnight. All your trades are executed within a single day, most of them within half an hour or even just a few minutes.

For the day trader, there is no tomorrow. Unlike an investor in a young tech company or a turnaround situation, you don't have the luxury of waiting around till the market recognizes the value that you've already seen in the business. You need to get in and out, fast. You never leave your money at risk overnight.

If you trade in the derivatives markets you may also come across *hedgers*. They will be using the same securities you're trading to hedge their holdings of stocks or commodities. Oil companies may hedge by selling oil ahead to lock in a favorable market price. Electricity companies may buy futures contracts of energy sources to reduce their input costs. Hedgers may be willing to take small losses on the derivatives in order to avoid much worse losses on the actual commodity - and one reason you can walk away with a profit!

Another way of looking at what traders do is to see their job as looking for volatility - prices rising or falling fast - and managing risk. The market will go up and down whether you're there or not. Your business is to jump in and out of market flows, piggy-backing them as long as they're going in the right direction. Sometimes you need to jump in just before a change of direction, so you need to read the whirls and eddies very carefully to see which way the river's flowing.

To do that, you'll need to have real self-discipline. A lot of our images of traders are swashbuckling - George Soros taking a $1bn position against the pound sterling and nearly "breaking the Bank of England" in 1992, Elon Musk putting money into Bitcoin, or The Big Short in which a bunch of traders brought the US mortgage securities market tumbling down.

In fact, these examples are the reverse of what day trading is. Soros and the fund managers who went short on the mortgage market based their actions on fundamental analysis, on detailed research about what was really going on. That's not trading - that's investing!

And no day trader would ever take a billion dollar position. Day traders are more interested in taking a few pennies out of Bath & Body Works when it bounces off a support level, or making a couple of percent out of Omega Healthcare when the market overreacts to its slightly below par results.

Because day trading profits are typically small profits, you need to make sure your losses are even smaller. That's one big reason that you need discipline. You need the discipline to set tight stop losses, and exit a trade the moment it stops working the way it's supposed to. You'll also need a trading strategy that doesn't let you go veering off after distracting great ideas from TikTok or Reddit that will lose you money, and you'll need to stick to it. Self-discipline and a good system are the only things standing between you and panic, greed, fear, and the deep red ink.

The other thing these great stories of 'trading' don't tell you is that as a day trader, you are not looking for that one great transformative trade that will pay off your home loan and let you retire somewhere with sunshine and pina coladas on tap. You will be looking for nine or ten trades a day. Some will lose, some will make a small return, and you are looking to manage your trading so that overall, you're ahead. That's not quite as exciting as it is in the movies, is it?

Myth and reality

The myths about day trading are everywhere. "It's exciting! You can get rich quick!"

"It's easy" - that's another one.

Day trading is not easy. It's not easy for me, and I've been doing it a while. It's even harder when you're getting started.

And you can't get rich quick, if you're using a good risk management system. For the first year or so, you'll be working hard for a relatively small return - though at the same time, you'll be keeping your hard-earned capital safe.

However, as the size of your trading book grows, you will be able to take on bigger trades without any extra risk. As you get more experience in day trading, you will refine your strategies and become more effective at executing them. After 18 months or a couple of years, your trading will start to bring in more and more profit as compounding works in your favor - reinvesting your trading profits in bigger trades.

The difficult thing is keeping yourself motivated until that happens.

Let's look at some more myths.

"Day trading is dangerous! You could lose all your money."

No doubt some people do, but they lose money because they don't trade with discipline. First of all, let me be very clear about this, you don't trade with money you can't afford to lose. You do not trade with money that's intended as downpayment on a home or that you need to pay your home loan or your bills or your medical insurance. You never, ever trade with "scared money." You trade with money that you could afford to lose.

And you always control the risk. In fact, if you always use stop losses properly, and if you always close your positions at the end of the trading day, and if you use a money management system (which I'll tell you about later), you're very unlikely to lose all your money. These are the boring things about trading, and the people who lose all their money skip over the boring bits when they read about how to trade profitably - or they decided to ignore them.

"You are only as big as your last trade." This can be useful to remember if you're getting cocky. But it's not actually true. Your success as a day trader will never be defined by a single trade but by your batting average - your day-to-day average success.

After all, no one sets up a hotel and then says "Success!" after *one* guest stays *one* night. You build a hotel to accommodate a large number of simultaneous guests over a long period of time. In the same way, trading is your business - it's not a single trade. You are only as big as your risk capital - the money in your trading account - and that depends on your win rate, profitability, and risk across all your trades.

"Trading is for alpha males who need to win."

Well first I should tell you some of the best traders I know are female. So that's one part of that myth demolished.

But you don't need a big ego to be a good day trader. You don't need to win every trade. You don't need to bet the bank. No one is watching your performance and no one expects you to put your house or your life on the line. And you know, your friends are considerably probably more interested in talking about the Superbowl, where you went on vacation or how your kids are doing in school than they are about how you cornered the market in silver futures.

Challenges and Rewards

Why day trade? It's actually not a bad lifestyle.

First off, you will be able to achieve financial prosperity. Okay, you could also meet this by being a top surgeon or owning five apartment buildings, or by inventing the app that everyone needs. But you don't need to have any certifications to day trade, the in-price is lower, and you don't need to code (though if you want to automate your trades, it helps).

If you're successful as a day trader, there is no limit to ambition. Even the most successful professionals eventually run up against salary limits. Equally, a top surgeon may well not be able to retire, even though there is good money coming in; as a day trader, you can attain financial freedom much more quickly.

If you have a career as a day trader, it promises you complete independence. You are responsible only to yourself (and perhaps your family). No boss complaining you were in two whole minutes late because your three-year-old is sick. No finance department sending you new targets for next month or complaining you didn't meet last month's targets. You make the rules!

There's no b.s. factor - you don't have to wear a suit or give PowerPoint presentations or learn the latest corporate jargon about low hanging fruit or being world class, or whatever. You don't need to be on-brand and no one is policing your social media profile. You are responsible for your own success, that's your one and only responsibility.

You can structure your trading life, whether it's three hours every morning, Asian markets overnight, or taking Wednesdays off. You can work from home, rent an office, be a digital nomad, or live in a cabin in the Adirondack Mountains or a chateau in France, as long as you have good internet access.

Of course the downside is that if you're your own boss living in a tropical paradise - which you could be - you're going to need the self-discipline to get up and trade the open every day, *before* you head to the pool or the cocktail bar!

The challenge, of course, is making winning trades and containing your losses.

In some ways, day trading is like dieting. Everyone's an expert, but no one gets any thinner. People day trade, but they never get richer. And the reason why is the same in both cases; a lack of self-discipline and the ability to lie to yourself.

If you're paper trading and you miss out on a few losing trades when you're calculating your return rate, you're lying to yourself. If you plan for a crazily high ratio of winning trades, you're lying to yourself. Just like if you're dieting and you say, "But one little Reese's Peanut Butter Cup isn't going to make me fat" … you're lying to yourself.

Another challenge, and I should be very clear about it right now, before you go any further, is boredom. Some people can't keep their attention on anything for more than a few minutes. You'll need to be able to track the market on a computer screen for hours at a time. Blink and you'll miss the best entry point for a great trade.

You will be stuck behind a desk, on your own, watching computer screens, for as long as it takes you to trade. That might be two hours. It might be all day. You will be looking at scanners full of numbers, and trying to make sense out of charts, and it can be mind-numbing.

It can also be the greatest way to earn a living, ever.

Why do most day traders fail?

Why do so many day traders flake out early in their careers? I think that fear has a lot to do with it.

They are afraid, because they are not comfortable with the idea of loss. But if you can't take a loss making trade, even a day that loses money, you will not become a successful trader. The fear will haunt you, and either make you feel anxious all the time (which is no fun at all), or push you into mistakes.

For instance, the fear of making a loss makes many beginner traders hang on to trades that are going wrong. Rather than lose a penny a share, they hang on to their positions and end up losing $2 a share. Other times, traders end up like a rabbit in headlights, looking all around but unable to actually do anything. "Paralysis by analysis" is another symptom of fear; not being quite ready to click the buy button, and looking at those charts again and again instead of entering the trade.

There's also FOMO - fear of missing out. The market starts to move, the trader's not quite ready, and then seeing the stock going up, the trader chases the stock price upwards and ends up buying at a price that's too high to make a good profit. Or second-guessing what would actually be a good trade, by worrying too much about the downside, or getting panicked by the market.

Some traders keep changing their strategy all the time. They're looking for the one "100% winning" strategy, which, by definition, cannot possibly exist. (In fact, you can lose more than half the time and still make money, if you exercise stop losses rigorously and ensure your risk/reward ratio is correct.)

Fear and greed push traders into emotional decision making when they should be using hard numbers and well planned and executed strategies. Some traders really want to get an adrenaline rush out of their trades; that's not conducive to good trading. There's a sort of magical thinking that can take over when things get stressful; your lizard brain is trying to kill and eat the market as if it was a sort of woolly mammoth. Of course, if you're using your human brain to think with, you know that nothing you do can change a losing trade.

The other thing that causes new traders to fail is that they don't run their trading as a business - which is what it is. If you start a business, you need a business plan. You need to define how much money you're risking, what kind of trades you plan to do, and how much profit you seek to make. You also need to test your trading strategies to be sure they work; that's where businesses use surveys, pilot projects, and focus groups, but you'll be using software systems and market prices.

You must have an edge

Every really successful business has an edge. Apple, Adidas, UFC, and Disney have an edge because they have fantastic brands. Amazon has an edge because it's made a huge investment in logistics, so it can deliver faster than virtually any other store. Warren Buffett's edge as an investor was doing his own very detailed and thorough research.

So, what is your edge going to be?

I can't tell you this; you're going to have to work it out yourself. But I can help you with the process of finding it.

Remember that the market is a continual tug-of-war between buyers and sellers, creating a continuous flow of price change. You need to find situations that deliver an advantage; you can recognize them by recognizing patterns that have created conditions for good trades in the past. Then you backtest, running your strategy against the market records for the last several years to see whether it would have worked.

What traders refer to as "edge" is all about getting the odds on your side. You're aiming to be like a casino - casinos pay out to gamblers all the time, but because they stack the odds in their own favour, they very rarely go bust. Like a casino, you won't win all the time, but your edge, or advantage, will play out over time, over a large number of trades.

"Edge" is actually quantifiable. For casinos, it's about 2%. For traders, it needs to be a good deal more, say 10-20% (I'll show you how to calculate it later). In many ways, it's more important than your win/loss ratio. You can lose a lot of trades if your edge is high.

Another thing you'll need to quantify is your risk/reward ratio. If you have a straight heads/tails flip, you're risking one to make one - a dollar lost if it's tails, a dollar won if it's heads. You need to win more than 50% of the time for this to work. But if you risk one to make three, you can lose two-thirds of your trades and still make money. Obviously, to do this you need to quantify both your expected profit and the amount of loss you are willing to take - and to stick to your guns and exit the trade if that loss happens.

You will need to develop your trading strategy and "edge" yourself. You could start with an idea; say, that the market often overreacts to news. Then start to think about how you could turn that idea into a trading strategy. And then backtest, to see if that strategy works, and find out how risky it is and how often you would win with it. Alternatively, you could start with one of the strategies suggested in this book, or you might find one that appeals in a chatroom or in a video.

But the important thing is that whatever this edge might be, you have to win *before* you start trading. You'll need to back-test the strategy, you'll need to have an idea of the possible danger points (some trades can be difficult to exit, others have a lot of false signals), and you'll need the discipline to execute your plan.

Preparation is key. Otherwise you're like an actor arriving on stage without having learned their lines.

What personality do you need to day trade with success?

Day trading isn't for everyone. Let's run through the qualities you'll need to make a successful trader.

First and foremost, you need to be self-disciplined. This is the downside of being responsible for your own success. If you can't manage to get out of bed in the morning, day trading is not for you.

You need to be independent and able to handle solitude. That doesn't mean "not being a people person" but it does mean being able to be on your own all morning without going off your head. If you really need the water cooler chat, or to be working in a team, day trading is not for you. (Although it *is* possible to join a trading team. Traders are social enough, but not generally when they are trading.)

You also need to be able to "turn off." It's important that you can close your trade station, go out bowling in the evening, relax with family at the weekend or go off hiking. If you're worrying about trades and markets all the time, day trading will kill you. If you have an addictive personality, its borderline; you need to prevent yourself from getting fixated on trading.

You need to be able to act fast and be decisive. You'll do research, but most of that is done before the markets open. Once you're trading, you need to be able to take a decision fast when you see a good opportunity open up. (You could, of course, set up an automated trade system for some types of trades. If you're a bit of a geek, that could be a rewarding style of business.)

And you need to be a good loser! Part of the discipline that makes good traders is drawing a line under a failed trade; they close it, make a small and controlled loss, and move on. They don't panic, they don't hold on hoping it will come good "real soon now," they don't feel angry or blame themselves - they just move on to the next trade. If you tick these boxes, you can be a successful day trader.

How much money do you need to begin trading?

Surprisingly, you do not need a lot of money to begin trading. Some brokers now accept just a few hundred bucks as an opening deposit, as do some forex and options platforms. Remember, though, that this needs to be risk capital, defined as money that you can lose without putting yourself in financial distress.

If you want to know whether it's risk capital, there are several ways to do so. One is to think about what would happen if your car needed a new gearbox, or if your home needed emergency repairs. Do you have some funds stashed away? Another is to think: if I took this money and blew it on a vacation, instead of putting it in this trading account, would I feel guilty or stupid?

Similarly, when you're trading, if you feel uncomfortable trading a certain amount, it's probably too much to put in a single trade. This is one time when I do think your gut feeling is worth consulting, and that's very rare in day trading.

There is one disadvantage to starting day trading with less than $25,000 in your account, if you are trading stock. It's the Pattern Day Trading rule. A Pattern Day Trader is defined by US law as someone who executes four or more 'round trip' deals (buying and selling on the same day) within five working days. Pattern Day Traders need to have $25,000 in the account. If you don't have $25,000, you will only be able to do three trades a week. However, these rules do not apply to futures or currency trading (unless it's in your equity brokerage account).

Why do you trade?

There is a simple answer to this. The one and only reason to day trade is: to make money!

Many losing traders get started for other reasons. They're trying to prove something to themselves, or they have a dream of being rich without making any effort.

Day trading, like any other business, is intended to make money. You'd buy a fast food franchise to make money, not because you want free burgers. You'd start a tech consultancy to make money, not to tax-expense your computer. You'd drive a taxi to make money, not because you enjoy driving. And so, you day trade to make money. It's as simple as that. It's a business. Treat it like a business, and it will work. Treat it as a fun hobby and it probably won't.

Just to check your understanding, every chapter in this book will have a short multiple-choice quiz at the end. Don't worry; no one's keeping the score, and you'll probably find that you do pretty well in most chapters. If you don't, all that's telling you is to re-read the chapter, maybe after a couple of days, and see if it makes better sense. The quiz answers are on page 272.

Chapter 1 Quiz

1. Which of these behaviours will lose you the most money?
   a) Drinking too much coffee
   b) Getting up late
   c) Holding a bad trade in the hopes it will get better
   d) Not trading if you don't see a good risk/reward ratio

2. You need to be all of these - except one - to be a great trader. Which is the odd one out?
   a) A math whizz
   b) Self-disciplined
   c) Independent
   d) A good loser

3. Which of these is not an advantage of the day trading lifestyle?
   a) You're only accountable to yourself
   b) You'll get a regular return
   c) You choose your own hours
   d) There's no limit to the money you could make

4. Which of these statements about day trading is true?
   a) It's incredibly dangerous
   b) You can get rich quick
   c) You need a big ego to compete
   d) You will get more profitable the longer you trade

5. What is your edge?
   a) The odds of your winning, on average over all your trades
   b) Otherwise known as 'love handles'
   c) Something you can fall off
   d) The wall between yours and the next cubicle

2

Chapter 2: Introducing the Trading Assets

In this book, I'm going to focus mainly on stocks, which is what I trade, but you may find other assets more conducive to making trading profits. A number of different financial assets can be traded, and they all have their nuances; their markets have their own different ways of doing things, too. You may find some suit you more than others.

First of all, let's define what makes a good day trading asset.

It needs to be liquid - that is, easy to trade. So it needs to trade frequently and in reasonable volume. For instance, around 13 million Coca-Cola shares are traded every day, making it a liquid asset. You should be able to buy and sell shares easily, and at the price shown. On the other hand, Newlake Capital, a real estate trust that's traded over the counter (not on one of the major stock exchanges), only trades an average of 25,000 shares a day, and you might find it difficult to execute a large order in the stock.

It needs to be tradable at low cost, including the spread (the difference between the price you can buy at and the price you can sell at, known as the bid and the ask price). If you have to pay high commissions to trade, that will be a drag on your performance and could even prevent you from making a profit.

The price needs to change on a regular basis so that you can trade; a stock that flatlines doesn't give you any chance to do so. In market speak, what you're looking for is volatility (and that can be calculated and screened for - I'll show you how later on).

Some traders also add the requirement that every stock they trade has to have a fundamental driver - that is, it's being driven upwards by good results, or downwards by a negative trend in the sector.

You may also have some other requirements. For instance, if you want to trade with leverage (the use of borrowed money to invest), you may want to use a broker who will let you open a margin account - which is when the broker lends you cash to purchase securities. You can then trade more stock than you have cash, giving you a potential higher return (but also, of course, increased risk).

If you have relatively small resources, you will need to look for assets that fit your position size (size of trade); for instance, in stocks, where a round lot (100 shares) is affordable. A round lot in Berkshire Hathaway would cost you over $40,000. A round lot in Vici Properties would cost you $2,900 - a big difference.

Stocks

A company stock entitles you to fractional ownership of the company's assets, earnings, and cash flow. It is a limited liability asset - you can only lose your investment, but you can't lose any more than you put in (unless you're trading on margin). Stocks trade in relation to the company's earnings prospects, so economic news, earnings releases, new products, and announcements from competitors or regulators, could all move the share price.

Shares are traded in round lots, that is, 100 shares or multiples of 100 shares. However, this isn't quite the difficulty that it used to be for traders with relatively small resources, since many brokers now offer smaller lots and even trade fractional shares. This is something you will need to check out when you are choosing your broker. Outside the US, some brokers let you trade CFDs (Contracts for Difference), but this is banned for US citizens.

When you're trading, you need to have a feel for the size of trade that can easily be filled in any particular stock. You can get this by looking at the trades that have gone through today (or yesterday, if you're planning to trade the opening). You'll find that some shares are easy to trade in lots of 100, but liquidity is tighter for larger trades, for instance 500 shares or more. This applies particularly to smaller stocks and those with less free float, and those with share prices in excess of $100 or so. Larger lots may be filled as long as volume is moving fast, but there is then always a possibility that getting out might be tricky.

Many brokers now offer commission-free trading. However, commission isn't the only cost of trading in shares. There is a *spread* between the price you can sell at and the price you can buy at, which is the market maker's mark-up. For instance, you can buy IBM for $187 but if you want to sell, you'll only get $186, a $1 spread that equals 0.5% of the share price. On the other hand, Iron Mountain (IRM) has a spread of $68.66 to $69.48. That's less than a dollar, but it adds up to more than 1% of the share price - that's a significant cost if you're aiming to make a 4% or 5% return on each trade.

You'll want to trade on the New York Stock Exchange (NYSE) and Nasdaq. Smaller exchanges and the OTC (Over-The-Counter) market do not have enough liquidity. You might also look at London, Tokyo, Euronext, and Deutsche Boerse in Germany.

You can either go long (buy a stock to make money when the price rises) or go short (sell a stock to make money when the price falls). Going long is easier to get started with; not all traditional brokers are happy to let you short a stock. For most trades, they will work both sides, but be exceptionally careful when you go short, as your liability is theoretically infinite. If you go long, the price can only fall to zero; if you go short, the price could double, treble, or go up ten times, and then you're really in trouble if you didn't execute your stop loss.

Bonds

A bond is, basically, an IOU. Bonds are issued by companies and governments who need capital. The investor who buys the bond is lending the company or government money who promises to pay the investor interest (coupons) for a certain period of time, and to repay the bond on a certain date (maturity). Bond issues can be huge. In 2023, the International Bank for Reconstruction and Development (IBRD) issued a $5 billion sustainability bond, and Pfizer issued a massive $31 billion.

Bonds, unlike shares, don't give any ownership to investors over a company's assets unless the company goes bust. If you buy US Treasury bonds you don't 'own' the US! They tend to trade in line with general economic news, and in inverse correlation to interest rates; that is, if the interest rate goes down, bond prices go up (and vice versa).

Bonds have two kinds of risk; there is interest rate risk, and there is default risk - what happens if an issuer can't, or decides not to pay the coupon, as Russia did in 1998. The default risk can be assessed by looking at the ratings issued by ratings agencies (Fitch, S&P, and Moody's); the best bonds will be given AAA and AA ratings (German government bonds are AAA, French and US bond AA). These ratings indicate the highest creditworthiness and lowest risk of default.

Besides US Treasuries, other tradable government bonds include

• OATS (France)

• Bunds (Germany)

• JGBs (Japan)

• Gilts (UK).

Bonds are not as frequently traded as equity, since large pension funds and insurance companies will sometimes buy a bond at issuance and hold it to maturity, in order to match their liabilities (payment of pensions, or of insurance claims). The interest payments received from the bond are predictable, which means a pension fund can cover its expected pension payments with them and be sure it will not be out of pocket. Apart from Treasuries and Gilts (which are listed on the London Stock Exchange), most other bonds trade over-the-counter, so there is no price quote, and no centralized market. Price volatility is not high, so it is relatively difficult to make a good return from day trading.

ETFs

You may be used to the idea of a mutual fund as a pool of money managed by a professional fund manager to buy into the market. An Exchange Traded Fund (ETF) is a similar pool, usually designed to replicate the performance of a particular market, sector, or commodity. Unlike mutual funds, though, ETFs are traded on the stock exchange, in the same way that shares are traded.

ETFs might replicate the performance of an index like the S&P 500 by buying each share in the index, in proportion to its size as part of the index (its weighting). In other cases, ETFs might use synthetic replication techniques, such as using derivatives to achieve a copy of the index's performance.

Not all ETFs have the same liquidity. Some of the sector ETFs and thematic ETFs, such as green energy, cannabis, and infrastructure ETFs may have quite low traded volumes. The most interesting ETFs for stock market traders will be the big index ETFs which copy the S&P and DJIA, the FTSE 100, Nikkei, CAC-40 in France, and DAX in Germany. The most popular with day traders is the S&P 500.

US-traded ETFs include

• SPY - SPDR 500 Trust, which mirrors the S&P 500

• DIA - Dow Jones Industrial ETF, which mirrors the 30 stocks in the DJIA

• QQQ - Invesco QQQ ETF, which copies the 100 top Nasdaq shares and has a high technology component.

Sector ETFs that might be worth considering include

• XLE - Energy Select SPDR

• SMH - VanEck Semiconductors ETFs.

And for major indexes outside the US:

• FXI - iShares China Large-Cap

• EWJ - iShares MSCI Japan

• FLEE - Franklin FTSE Europe

• SPEU - SPDR Portfolio Europe.

Some ETFs offer a leveraged play on the indexes. For instance, TQQQ offers three times the QQQ's returns (both up *and* down), and QLD offers twice the QQQ. However, if you're going to trade these you need to take on board the high level of risk involved. Personally, I don't like leveraged ETFs much. I'd prefer to take my leverage by using a margin account to trade the straight ETF.

You might also want to look at commodities ETFs like

• USO - United States Oil Fund, and

• GLD - SPDR Gold Trust.

Ensure you know what you're getting, as some ETFs copy the performance of oil shares and gold shares, not the actual commodities.

And finally, a bond ETF that might be worth looking at is TLT, the iShares 20+ Year Treasury Bond ETF.

Before you decide to trade an ETF (or invest in one!), always check the tracking error. Sometimes, the ETF doesn't track the index it's based on very well. If I want to replicate the performance of an index or a commodity, I can do 'physical replication', i.e. I actually buy, let's say, bars of gold bullion and store them, or I can do synthetic replication by, let's say, writing swaps contracts and futures contracts that will deliver the same performance. Which is all good in theory, but very rocket scientist intensive, and if you get it wrong for any reason, you could outperform or underperform the index you are trying to copy. For instance you might have overlooked a currency mismatch, bought futures that were too high risk, had trading costs that were too high...

On the other hand, if you actually own the gold (or shares, or barrels of oil) then your performance will be an exact copy. This is why tracking error is one of the things you really need to look at when analyzing ETFs, because some do a better job than others. For instance, the United States Oil Fund (USO) doesn't always track the price of crude oil accurately because it uses futures contracts rather than tracking the spot price with actual purchases of oil.

Since futures contracts reflect expectations about moves in the price, they can vary widely from the spot price today.

Currency

Foreign exchange represents a massive and highly liquid market that never stops, with trillions of dollars traded every day. It's a bigger market than either the stock market or the bond market - or indeed both of them added together.

What's slightly different about the currency market is that it's traded in currency *pairs*, since each currency is quoted against another. For instance, USDJPY quotes dollars to yen, while 'cable' quotes dollars to pound sterling, a slang for the GBPUSD currency pair. The main currencies suitable for trading are the US dollar, Euro, Yen, Pound Sterling, and Swiss Franc. But you might also find less well-known pairs that are interesting to trade, like Australian dollar to Sterling, Hong Kong Dollar to USD, or the Canuck/Yankee combination of Canadian dollar to USD.

Remember which way round the quote works. The first currency is the base currency, or numerator: it's always worth one. So, in USDGBP, you're trading one dollar, and the second currency is what you get for it. USDGBP is currently trading at 0.79, that is, you get £0.79 for $1.00.

There are spot rates for currencies, but you can also trade currency futures or even currency ETFs. Currency can be traded on margin, at 10:1 or even 50:1 leverage. Price changes in currencies are given in pips - the fourth decimal place. Always be aware of the effect of a single pip movement on your total position size.

If you're trading the spot markets, you need to know that there is no organized exchange; it's a free-for-all of banks, traders, hedge funds, dealers and brokers. You will also need to open a dedicated currency account to trade. In return, you have huge flexibility of trading size - and unlike futures, no expiration dates to worry about.

Commodities

Commodities are basic goods, such as metals, wheat, or oil. Now, obviously, you as a day trader don't want to be buying physical products, so you'll just day trade the futures contracts or perhaps ETFs. A big company *might* want a hedge against one of their major costs rising, and be prepared to take physical delivery of a load of wheat or steel, but traders simply want to make money without having to buy the physical goods.

A futures contract is a promise. If you buy a contract, you are basically saying you *will* buy the goods at the price you pay. Now be careful, because you only want to trade that contract, you don't want to take on the delivery. Futures are a kind of derivative, that is, a financial contract whose value is related to that of an underlying asset (a commodity, stock, or index).

Futures contracts are standardized, and you will most probably start off trading one contract. For instance, corn is traded in contracts representing 5,000 bushels, though it is *priced* in bushels; oil contracts represent 1,000 barrels of oil. Each contract has an expiration date (when you don't want to be left holding the baby); some are monthly, others quarterly. You'll see the expiry date in the description - "December 2024 corn" for instance. Before one contract expires, a new contract will already have started, on what's called rollover day; you'll want to jump ship from trading the nearly expired contract to trading the newly-launched one as soon as the trading volume in the market shifts to the new contract.

Futures prices reflect expectations about the future, so they may be quite different from the spot price (current market price).

Futures have longer trading hours than stocks or bonds. The stock market doesn't trade on weekends, but the S&P e-mini (a stock futures contract) does. You'll need to put up 5-15% of the contract size as your initial margin.

Each type of contract has its own tick size, the minimum price change. For instance, the tick for crude is $0.01 a barrel, so a move for a 1,000-barrel contract can be as small as $10. Smaller tick sizes are to your advantage. Larger tick sizes are to your disadvantage; the $12.50 tick is one of the downsides of the S&P e-mini.

Mini and micro contracts were specially developed to appeal to retail traders like you and me, offering a smaller size than the standard futures contracts. Let's take an example, the Nasdaq 100.

• NDA: contract size = $100 x Nasdaq index points

• ENQ - Nasdaq e-mini: contract size = $20 x Nasdaq index points

• MNQ - micro Nasdaq: contract size = $2 x Nasdaq index points.

Futures have one big advantage. Unlike stocks, they are not subject to the wash-sale rule, which can be an advantage for 'amateur' traders (as defined by the IRS). In a wash sale, a trader sells a security at a loss for tax benefits and then purchases the same or a similar security within 30 days, before or after the transaction. However, futures can be much more volatile and higher risk than stocks, as futures trading is highly leveraged and commodity prices often experience large swings and extreme cyclicality.

Types of derivative

Futures contracts are one type of derivative, but you can also trade options contracts. Unlike futures, options do not oblige the holder to purchase the underlying assets; they give the holder the right (but not the obligation) to buy or sell the underlying asset at a given price (strike price or exercise price), up to a particular date in the future (expiry). If exercising the option won't make you any money, you can simply let it expire. Most options traded are options on shares, or on stock indexes.

'Call' options give you the right to buy a share at the exercise price; 'put' options give you a right to sell.

"One Apple June 160 call" for instance gives you the right to buy 100 Apple shares at $160, up to the end of June. Apple is currently trading $183, so those options are in theory, worth $183 - $160 = $23 a share, times 100 shares = $2,300, *before* the time value is taken into account. This is the intrinsic value (real value) of the option.

Options are a wasting asset - that is, they have a time value, but as they approach the expiry, that value diminishes. You can imagine that if you still held that June 160 call an hour before it expires, but Apple had fallen to $150, then your option wouldn't be worth anything - you could buy the shares at $150 in the market, so why pay $160 with your option?

Traded options are standardized, with strike prices in regular increments; each option covers 100 shares. The length of options may differ; they may be weekly, monthly or longer. You can trade options on SPY and QQQ, for instance; these are large and liquid, just what you want as a day trader.

You may also find warrants and convertible bonds on some stocks. Companies issue warrants, which give the holder the right to subscribe for shares in the company at a given price in the future. They work in a similar way to options, and they're valued using the same methods. Companies also issue convertible bonds, which can be exchanged for stock at a given price. These combine elements of a bond and an option, and are traded on the stock exchange. However, in many cases they may not be liquid enough for you to day trade.

The two important things to realize about derivatives are that they have a limited life span, and that they are leveraged. Both these features represent added risk and you need to be sure you understand them.

For instance, a stock trading at $110 will lose you $10 if it falls to $100. If it goes up to $120 you'll gain $10 per share.

However, an option to buy the same stock that trades at $110 for $100 will be worth $10. But if the stock falls to $100 and you hold the option, not the stock, you will be wiped out - a ten percent loss in the stock equals a one hundred percent loss on the option (give or take the time value).

On the other hand, if the stock goes up to $120, your option will likely double (100% gain), whereas the stock will only make you $10.

Brokers will generally allow new traders rather limited choices. To day trade options, you'll need level 2 access, which offers complete access to the order book, showcasing the detailed buy and sell orders behind a stock's current market prices (level 1 is just for hedging stock). Further levels allow more sophisticated options strategies, and eventually, writing naked options (a much higher level of risk). You should note that trading options falls under the Pattern Day Trader rules which I discussed in chapter 1.

The exchanges on which you can trade derivatives are CBOE, and CBOT, NYMEX and CME (the last three are all part of the same group).

Cryptocurrencies

Cryptocurrencies such as Bitcoin are a relative newcomer to the world of day trading. These virtual currencies are tradable at a fairly low cost. They are also often volatile, giving good trading opportunities. You can day trade cryptocurrencies on eToro brokerage, but you might also use a crypto exchange such as Binance, Coinbase, or Kraken.

Understanding 'the law of one price' and arbitrage

You have probably been told to "Buy low, sell high." That makes trading seem very easy. What's less easy is knowing whether the price you see right now is low or high! In fact, as a trader, you need to recognize that, basically, the market is right, and the market sets the price.

The law of one price says that the *same asset* is worth the *same everywhere*. IBM isn't worth $184 in New York and $100 in London or $299 in Tokyo. It isn't even worth $184 in New York and $185.50 in London. Financial markets nowadays are too closely connected and too transparent for this kind of mispricing to happen on a regular basis.

Arbitrage takes advantage of times when the law of one price, momentarily, isn't working. For instance, if you get the chance to buy an option that's priced at less than its intrinsic value, that's an arbitrage. Or perhaps one pension fund in London decided to sell all of its holdings in Shell. It might take a few seconds for all the traders in New York to realize and do their sums, so there might be an arbitrage between the shares and the ADRs (the form in which foreign shares are traded in the US).

Day traders used to do well out of arbitrage, which is low or even no risk. However, arbitrage lends itself to automation, and that means the high-frequency traders, using algorithmic trading on super-powered computers, are exploiting most of the good opportunities these days. They can trade in and out quicker than you can click the button on a buy order. (They also sometimes create "flash crashes" with sudden huge volatility, something you might take advantage of.)

Pure arbitrage is riskless: you buy and sell at the same time in different markets, or through different securities. But you might also use risk arbitrage which is an investment strategy used during takeover deals, and has greater returns. It still involves offsetting two investments, but those might be, for instance, an acquisition target and the acquirer. In simple words, you profit from the difference between the target stock's market price and the acquirer's valuation of the shares. You sell one and buy the other to exploit the fact that the target has shot up and the company buying it has seen its stock fall. However, risk arbitrage trades usually need time to work out, and are more suited to swing trading (where a position can be taken for two or three days) rather than day trading.

Making your choice of assets

When you are choosing what to trade, it's important to find focus. Starting off day trading currency and stocks and commodities all at the same time is the kind of scatter-gun approach that will make you losses because you're not focused enough. You need to define which market you're going to be in.

You don't want to define it too narrowly, either. Just day trading IBM would mean you'd sit things out most days because you wouldn't see an ideal trade. You might select stocks; you might even trade two markets, for instance, if Asian market hours suit you.

If you have existing knowledge of a particular market, for instance because you are already an investor in stocks, that might mean the stock market is easier for you to trade, compared to commodities or currencies where you'll have to learn everything from scratch. That's how I got started day trading the stock market. If you already know crypto, and have been involved in that market for a while, then that might be a good place to start. But remember, being a day trader is different from being an investor or a trend follower.

Pick markets that are open when you want to trade - particularly if you prefer to trade early mornings or late evenings.

Choose markets that are accessible with your level of capital. Using micro or mini lots to trade currency or S&P futures is the best choice if your funds are limited, for example. If you have over $25,000, day trading stocks is a great choice. And make sure the markets you choose are liquid enough to trade without slippage (i.e. paying higher entry prices and having to sell below the market price to exit the trade).

During the rest of this book I'm going to talk mainly about the stock markets, because those are the markets where I trade the most and have the most knowledge. But the lessons of how to set up a trading system, how to read price formations on charts, and how to spot profitable opportunities, are common to all the different markets mentioned in this chapter.

Chapter 2 Quiz

1. What does it mean when we call an asset liquid?
   a) Well, it's liquid, like hot chocolate or water
   b) It's easily tradable at low cost and at any time
   c) It is tax-efficient
   d) It has to be traded on an official exchange

2. What is an ETF?
   a) An Emerging Trust Fund
   b) An Equivalent That's Fungible
   c) An Exchange Traded Fund
   d) An Easy Transaction Fix

3. Which of these is not a tradable commodity?
   a) Pork bellies
   b) Gold
   c) Pokemon cards
   d) Cocoa

4. What is a derivative?
   a) A share in a company that doesn't pay a dividend
   b) When you copy another trader's idea
   c) A special class of municipal bond
   d) A financial instrument based on an underlying security

5. What is arbitrage?
   a) Taking advantage of different prices for the same asset
   b) A hostile takeover
   c) Trading an asset in a different currency
   d) The French name for a referee

3

Chapter 3: How the Financial Markets Work

Daily life has sanitized the markets most of us use. We go to the supermarket and we pay the sticker price. We fill up with gas and we pay what it says on the pump. And we get along just fine with that.

But that's not how financial markets work. In financial markets, a price is part of a discussion between buyers and sellers. You may see a price on the screen, but it's not like a supermarket sticker price - it could suddenly change, in either direction, in response to news, a big sale of stock, a recommendation by a major investment firm, the way the charts look, or a change in the direction of the market as a whole.

So, let's take a look at how the markets work. While the details may differ between markets, all financial markets work in a similar way, which is more like a load of auctions going on at the same time than like a supermarket.

Stock market basics

Wall Street began not with a skyscraper, but with a tree - a sycamore tree in the street that had been named after the wall that the Dutch built to keep the British out. (That worked well, didn't it?) It was here that traders gathered to buy and sell the first US government bonds. Imagine a sort of securities flea market or bring-and-buy and you wouldn't be far wrong. Then, in 1827, the New York Stock Exchange opened at Wall and Hanover Streets. It's been trading ever since.

And although markets went from the tree to the stock exchange building, and then from the trading floor to electronic order fulfillment, keeping those founding fathers of the stock market in your mind gives you a good feeling for how financial markets work. There are buyers, and there are sellers. Buyers push the price up if they get control of the market, and sellers push the price down when they're in control.

While there are, by definition, as many buyers as sellers because someone has to sell the stock for someone else to be able to buy, one or the other side will generally be making more headway. The buyers are 'bulls' and the sellers are 'bears' (so a 'bear market' is one where the sellers are pushing prices downwards, and a 'bull market' is roaring away upwards). It's a teeter-totter, the stock market, and it doesn't take much to unbalance the seesaw.

In the days when you could just turn up at the tree and shout out what you wanted to buy, it was easy to access the market. But in today's sophisticated markets it's not that easy - there are thousands of investors and traders wanting to do so. Different markets link all these participants together in different ways; although you'll go through a broker, how your broker accesses the market will vary.

NYSE, for instance, has *specialists* - or had; as they are now called Designated Market Makers, or DMMs. Each stock has its own specialist, who runs the auction in that stock (and probably a number of others). They also hold stock so that they can provide liquidity when the market is moving fast, and there is high demand. However, they no longer have 'posts' on the trading floor; orders are handled electronically.

Nasdaq, on the other hand, allows any number of different market makers to make bids and offers on stocks in competition with each other. Goldman Sachs, Citadel Securities, and Credit Suisse, for instance, will all quote their own prices. And there are also ECNs, electronic communications networks that put buyers and sellers in touch with each other.

Efficient market theory

Economists have always been fascinated by how the market works, and came up with the efficient market theory to explain it. This says that the market is efficient; the price of a stock *always* reflects the sum total of knowledge about the stock. The market price is always right.

However, the market has small inefficiencies. For instance, it may overreact to earnings announcements, or one major seller might temporarily depress the price. But in these cases, you need to act fast to take advantage.

As a day trader, you are not really worried about whether the market is 'right' to value Microsoft at $404 a share. What you're looking at is what is going to happen to that share price as a result of supply and demand in today's trading session. What an *investor* wants to know about a stock is the business the company is involved in, its expected earnings and cash flow growth, and the assets it owns (both physical and intellectual). But what a *trader* wants to know about a stock is how it normally trades, in what volumes, with what spread, and whether it tends to trade within a particular price range.

What *both* the trader and the investor need to know, though, is the expected dates of major results, presentations, economic statistics and decisions that affect the stock. You don't want to get caught out by a big earnings surprise, or when the market is flattened by the Fed (Federal Reserve) putting interest rates up.

Risk and return

Day trading is not gambling and you shouldn't play hunches. You should always know exactly the risks you are running, and make sure those risks are stacked in your favor. You should know exactly what return you aim to make with a trade. If you can't quantify it, don't trade.

Risk and return are always related. Generally, an investment that is 'safe' will not have a great return. Stick your money in the bank, and you'll get interest every year - but not a lot of it. On the other hand, start-up companies can deliver impressive returns stacking up to many times the initial invested capital, but the risk is also significant - ten percent will fail in the first year, and another 70 percent won't make it past year five. The key to becoming a good trader is to understand the balance, and to spot opportunities to trade where the potential return is greater than the risk.

What is risk? Risk is the quantifiable likelihood of a negative event. Quantifying bad outcomes is what insurance companies do all the time, as well as risk managers within large enterprises; they use statistics to assess the risk of a house in a given neighborhood being burgled, or a shortage of raw materials, or a power outage at a particular data center. They then adjust the premiums their clients need to pay according to their assessment of the risk.

With a trade, you quantify the risk by deciding on a stop loss price - that is, a price at which you know the trade is not working out, and you will definitely exit. Don't worry, for each trade there's a way to do this, which I'll describe when we get to trading strategies. You also quantify the potential return. So, for instance, I may buy a stock at $20, expecting it to go to $22. That's my profit target. I will sell out if it goes to $19. So I am risking one dollar to get two.

It's no good just looking at the risk, or just looking at the reward - you need to look at both together, and have a reasonable idea of their probability. That is the essence of trading.

Note for paperback readers: You'll be seeing the charts in black and white. It just costs way too much to print them all in color. But you need to see them in color - that's the way you'll be seeing the charts you look at on your computer screen, and if you have three moving averages, for instance, you need to be able to tell which is which.

Therefore, I would recommend you please go to my website: www.az-penn.com and enter your best email address that I should send the colored images document to.

Volatility

Volatility is day traders' bread and butter. Volatility is the amount that prices vary over time. In very simple language, you want to buy a share that goes up and down a lot, giving you plenty of opportunities to trade; a share with high volatility.

There's a statistical way to find these stocks and that's by using standard deviation. The math may not mean much to you, but if you've seen a Bell curve chart (as shown below), you'll know how it works. For instance, if you charted the height of your male friends, you'd find most of them were in the middle of the chart around 5 feet 9 inches tall; there would be quite a lot at 5'6" and 6'2"; but there would be very few at 5'2" and 6'6". One statistician described a typical Bell curve to me as "looking like a python that swallowed a sombrero."

What standard deviation measures is the difference between each individual statistic and the average. You could apply it to your friends, but when you're trading you apply it to all the prices or returns from a given stock. A volatile stock is one that has a greater variation in returns (i.e. a greater difference from the average) than a less volatile one.

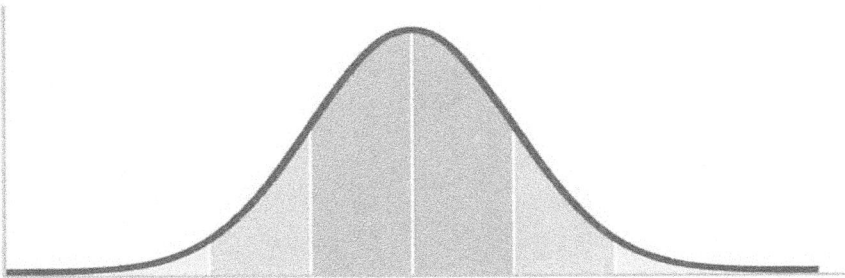

Take this a little further, with stocks, and you might want to see whether, say, Tesla is more or less volatile than the stock market as a whole. To do this you use what's called a beta. The benchmarket is the beta of the market, which is (by definition) one. A beta of more than one means a stock is more volatile than the market - it will go up more in an uptrend, and go down more in a downtrend, than the overall market. Though there's a formula for working out betas, thankfully you don't have to use it as most financial information sites such as Yahoo Finance will give you the figure. For Tesla, it's 2.41 - very significantly higher than the market. A look at Tesla's last five year chart below tells you why!

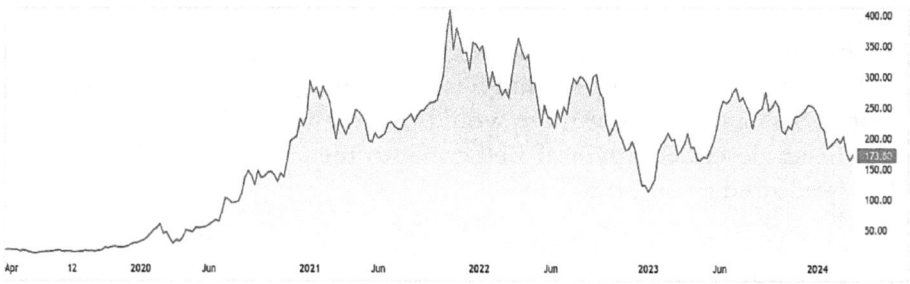

A high-beta stock is good for trading; the price will move up and down more often. On the other hand, a low-beta stock won't move much at all, and it's difficult (though not impossible) to make money trading stocks that don't go up or down. Take a look at the Walmart share price chart below, and you see a much less jagged outline with fewer big rises and falls. Walmart has a beta of just 0.34.

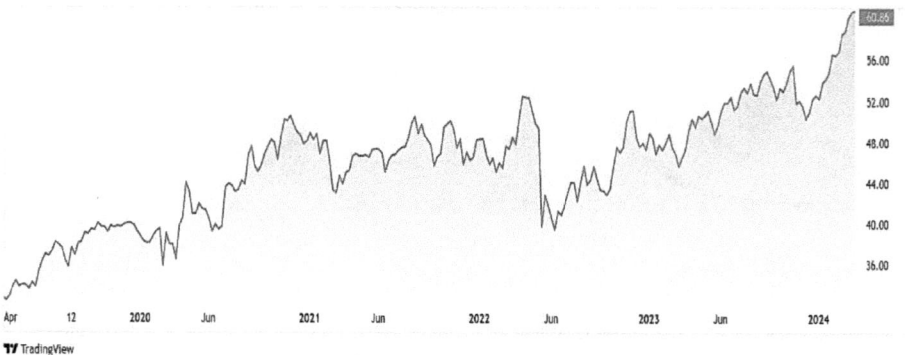

Opportunity cost

Although this is not as crucial to making money trading as the risk/reward ratio, you need to think about the opportunity cost of your trades. This means thinking about what else you might be doing with your time or money, instead of making a trade.

For instance, your money would make maybe 2.5% annually if you put it into a CD ladder at a bank. If you don't make more than 2.5% with your trading strategy, you are losing out. In fact, because trading puts your money at risk, you need to make several times 2.5% return to compensate for the risk. Or maybe, you'd make $1,000 a month if you applied your spare time to running a dog-walking business, rather than trading. So obviously, you'll need to make more than that trading for it to be a good business for you.

There is a very specific opportunity cost that traders and investors use to work out whether they are doing things right, and this is the *risk-free rate*. If you didn't take any risk at all, what return would you make?

Usually, the risk-free rate is assessed as being the interest rate on three-month US Treasury bills since it has almost no risk of default as they are backed by the US government. According to MarketWatch, it's currently sitting at 5.35%. If you don't make that, forget trading!

That said, if all your winning trades aim to make a couple of percent and you have a reasonable win/loss ratio, you will never make less than the risk-free rate.

The market's day

I didn't know certain things when I started trading, even though I thought my experience as an investor would help. For instance, when does the most stock trading happen in the day?

The opening is almost always the most active time. While futures stay open overnight, volumes of S&P futures reflect the stock market, and volumes overnight are usually low, making the market not ideal for traders. So, if you want the best chance of profit, hitting the New York Open is a must. Unfortunately, if you live on the West Coast, you will have to get up early to do so.

At the open, you will get some excitement from stocks 'gapping' up, as they reflect news overnight or before the open. There is a session of pre-market trading, but I use that for information rather than making trades; it can be very illiquid and is dominated by the big guys. (There's after-hours trading too, but I leave that alone, for the same reasons.)

Usually, there's some good trading volume later in the morning, too. The stock market takes a long lunch, with not much happening. In the afternoon, market makers are generally thinking about what they want their closing positions to look like, and the market will often trade in line with the existing trend - you won't get so many reversals of direction.

If you trade currencies, you'll find that forex trades rotate around the world. The Asian opening session focuses on JPY pairs, and you can trade Aussie or New Zealand dollars, but this isn't a great time to trade Canadian dollars or Swiss Francs, for instance. If you find the right currency pairs for the time slot, you'll have more flexibility in when you trade, as well as probably making better trades.

Market psychology

If you're trading, you're taking on the market. Whichever financial market you're in, it will work the same way. It's a big beast, and you need to know a lot about its typical behavior and reactions, or you risk being gobbled up for its next meal.

The market being made up of buyers and sellers, it reflects the psychology of crowds. You get groupthink, and you get panic reactions. At the extreme, you get the tech boom, the Tulip Boom and Bust of seventeenth-century Amsterdam, the 1929 Wall Street Crash. More often, you get standard market cycles, which can be described as having four stages: accumulation, markup, distribution, and markdown.

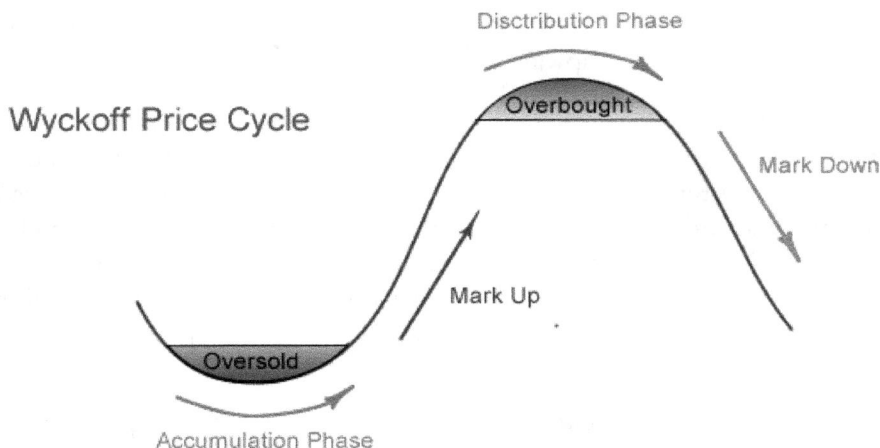

Distribution Phase

Wyckoff Price Cycle

Overbought

Mark Down

Mark Up

Oversold

Accumulation Phase

Accumulation happens at the end of a downtrend, and represents a foundation being laid. Buyers begin to accumulate the stock. There is more demand for the stock. The last sellers from the downtrend decide to exit the market. Eventually, all the overhang of stock has been taken up.

The markup phase begins when the overhang has gone; smart money and big institutions drive up demand, and now prices start to rise as well. The volume of stock being traded increases.

The distribution phase sees demand remaining strong, but now, some sellers are taking their profits. This increases the supply of the stock, and the price may start to move sideways rather than up. Eventually, there are too many sellers flooding the market with their stock.

This leads to markdown - demand for the stock wanes. There may be a final sudden spike on very high volume before the price starts to fall. Now, the market is in a downtrend, which will last till the next accumulation phase begins.

Market cycles can last for years. The bull market that began in March 2009 lasted 11 years. But there are cycles within cycles. A bull market will have plenty of what are called corrections, when it trades downwards for a while - these are mini-cycles. Even in a single day, you can see tiny cycles as a stock zooms up, then the sellers come out, and the price stalls and then falls. Or as a stock falls, then the buyers think it's a bargain, and suddenly the price starts to move upwards, fast.

The result of all these mini-cycles is that although markets will typically trade in an uptrend or downtrend, prices don't move smoothly. Instead, they move in zig-zags or steps. In an uptrend, each step will have a higher high, and a higher low; in a downtrend, lower highs and lower lows are the rule (as shown below). It's easy to see on a stock chart; it looks like a slightly wonky staircase.

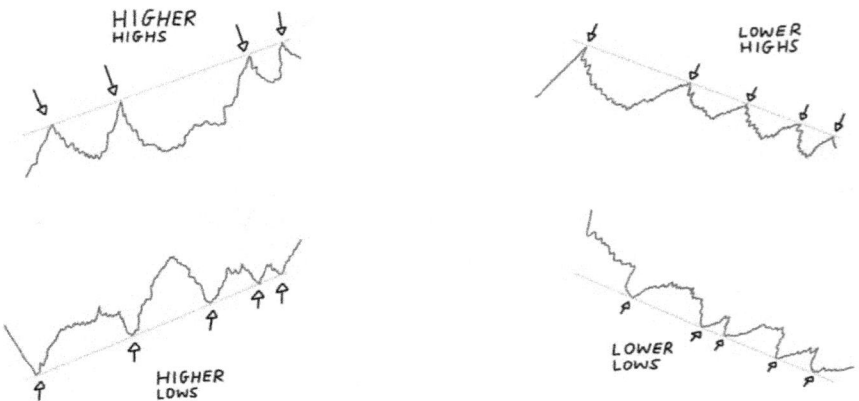

Within a trend, price movements going with the trend are usually stronger than those going against the trend. Price movements can also be categorized as action or reaction move; a *reaction* is usually limited to two-thirds the size of the existing *action* move, like waves going back down the beach. At the end of strong price movements you usually find a period of consolidation, when the market is balanced between buyers and sellers, with sideways or perhaps choppy price action as neither bulls nor bears win the day.

By the way, parabolic stocks - that is, stocks that are headed almost vertically upward - are terrifically exciting, but you should probably stay clear of them. What goes straight up very often goes straight down again. If you do want to trade really fast-moving stocks, you need to be careful about your setups; buying on a pullback, and using a small position size to get in, then scaling up as you go, with very tight stop losses.

Take a look on the next page at Tesla in late 2021. Bullish candlesticks kept marching up and up. Initially, there's a 45-degree curve during mid-2021, but then the stock price goes straight up. "We have a liftoff!" But if you had bought into that run upwards, you would have needed to be able to exit the stock before it crashed. And parabolic stocks don't often give you a good signal to get out. Buying into the run was a trade that could get flipped very, very quickly!

BATS:TSLA, 1W O168.76 H184.25 L168.73 C179.04 +8.21 (+4.81%)
Vol 168.505M

These stocks offer high reward, which is why we feel our hearts go all a-flutter when we look at the price charts - but they also present a very high risk, so take care.

Chapter 3 Quiz

1. How can a trader best manage risk?
   a) By setting a stop-loss on every trade
   b) By never trading more than their net worth
   c) By only trading NYSE stocks
   d) By not trading on Tuesdays

2. What does a beta tell you?
   a) Whether a company has a stable business
   b) How likely a stock is to go up
   c) The relationship between the stock's price action and the market's
   d) That a stock is not an alpha

3. Which of these would you *not* find in an uptrend?
   a) Higher highs
   b) Higher lows
   c) Higher highs and lows
   d) Lower lows

4. What happens during the accumulation phase?
   a) Companies issue more stock
   b) Governments issue more debt
   c) The overhang of stock that investors want to sell disappears
   d) Nothing

5. What is a parabolic stock?
   a) One that shows a steeper and steeper upwards price curve
   b) One that has a good 'story' to tell
   c) One that has options issued on it
   d) One with a high beta

4

Chapter 4: Tools and Platforms to Get Started

So now you know quite a lot about the different assets you could trade, and how to trade them, and what life could be like as a day trader. But now it's time to look at the practicalities - the nuts and bolts of day trading. You're going to need a broker, a trading platform, an office (even if it's your garage) and some basic infrastructure. Let's talk you through how to choose the right tools to get up and running.

This is a business not a computer game

Think about day trading as a business. It needs a business plan, and it needs some investment in basic business facilities. Building the right infrastructure for your business is important, and it will take you a good deal of work to get it right.

For instance, to make money day trading you need to be well in control of your costs. If your broker charges you too much commission, or can't execute your trades accurately, you won't reach your target profitability.

You also need to have realistic goals. "$5,000 a day real soon now" is not realistic. Don't set a money amount, but work through how many trades you expect to make, what your starting risk capital will be, and what profitability and what win/loss rate you expect.

What brokers to use

Long term investors are often not very choosy about their brokers. They might trade once or twice a month, so they don't worry if the order system is a bit clunky. They are looking to hold the stock for a good while, maybe for years, so they don't care if they always pay a bit of slippage because their broker doesn't get them absolutely the best price in the market, or trade *this very second* but maybe a couple of minutes later. They don't need a broker that can handle order sends order (OSO) and order cancels order (OCO).

Traders, on the other hand, need to be very, very choosy about their brokers. You need to get your orders filled at the right price in seconds, every single time. And you *also* need a broker that has reasonable costs. If you're being charged $25 a trade, you'll never be able to make money, however good your strategy and however high your win rate. If, at the same time, your broker lets you day trade with a tax-exempt account, you are home and dry.

Traders may also be interested in brokers who will give them margin. Many brokers will give you three times leverage or more; so if you have a $25,000 account, you can trade up to $75,000. I'd suggest you don't start to use margin till you have at least a few months' experience of day trading and feel fully confident that you are in control of your downside.

Maybe you're already an investor and you have a broker who meets your needs *as an investor.* Think twice before trying to *trade* on that platform. You may find that your broker has a separate trading platform and different account level that would give you what you need; if so, you will need to move up to that level, which may involve paying subscriptions. It's also best if you can separate your trading account from your investment account - this will help you greatly with tax issues and record keeping.

A few choices that might be interesting are:

• Interactive Brokers, which is inexpensive and also lets you have tax-free trading accounts;

• Charles Schwab's Thinkorswim platform;

• Webull, a cheap platform that might suit the beginner (but doesn't offer backtesting or automation);

• Mondeum, which is a low priced broker-dealer with good order fills, specifically designed for retail traders.

Ideally you need a broker with a good trading platform that can use hotkeys (we'll talk more about it later). You don't need to go through a whole process of loading the stock page, entering your trade manually, pressing a button, confirming the trade, and... whoops, the stock has moved and the trade is no longer attractive! You just have hotkeys to do all that.

A really good broker should offer you direct access to the markets. Direct access routing gives you more control and faster fills, which can add a small margin to your profitability, and means you're not going to see trades fail when the price moves too fast.

Trading platforms

Some brokers have their own platforms, like Interactive Brokers' Trader Workstation, and Charles Schwab, but you can also integrate a specialized trading platform to your broker. In fact, many traders find Trader Workstation too clunky, and spring for a separate platform.

DAS Trader is a good trading platform (as screenshotted below); some brokers will offer it as part of the account setup, while at others you'll have to pay a monthly subscription of $100-200. The ease of placing your orders and the speed and accuracy of execution make it worthwhile.

You might also consider RealTick EMS, TradeStation Securities, eSignal, CyberTrader or MetaStock.

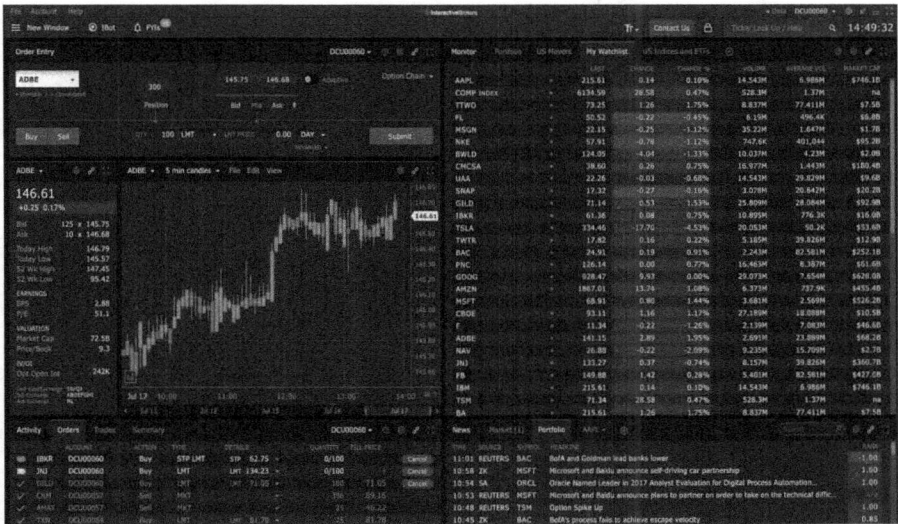

Make sure your trading platform gives access to all the relevant exchanges and ECNs. You also want to spec out:

• the reliability of the platform

• whether 24/7 support is available

• the speed of execution

• a user-friendly interface

• whether you can put all your important tools on a single page

• whether it is user-configurable

• whether you can customize your own charts

• how you are able to track your trading book overall

• how it manages watch lists and stock scanners

• whether it offers program alerts

• whether it offers stock futures access as well as just stocks.

And finally, of course, you need to go through the tariffs with a tooth comb.

It's actually worth taking time to go to a trading conference so you can see the different trading platforms in action, and maybe get to try them out. There is no better way to decide on which system to get than to take it for a test drive. For instance, TradersEXPO, Las Vegas, is in February, both free and paid options (but you have to pay your way there and your hotel of course); Forex Traders Expo and Summit Dubai, in May: London Trader Show in November, from £25 to £129 British Pounds. Many trading gurus also run their own. However, for some shows, the pricing information is not transparent and the detail of the presentations is unclear, so do proper research before attending.

A.Z Penn

Nasdaq Level 2 and bid/ask

Nasdaq Level 2 is a subscription service that gives you live access to the Nasdaq order book.

Level 1, which you'll see with any broker, just shows the National Best Bid and Best Offer (NBBO). That's the best price you can sell at, and the best price you can buy at. That's good information for an investor, but it won't show you market depth - how many buyers and sellers there are at that price. With Level 2, you can see all the market makers for a given stock, which lets you assess the demand for a stock much more accurately. You'll see the NBBO, but you'll also see the queue behind the NBBO - the 'next best' prices.

You can also see what size buyers and sellers are trading in, so that you can tell the difference between a stock with one market maker willing to meet small orders at a particular price, and a stock with a big sell order stacked up and ready to go.

Level 2 also shows prices from ECNs (electronic communication networks) which can link buyers and sellers automatically. This might help you refine your trade execution. If there is a big seller waiting with a line of stock, and you want to go long, you might want to wait till most of their shares have been bought up. That removes an influence that is keeping the share price down, so you are likely to be getting in at just the right point.

You can also get direct access to the ECNs through Level 2. That's just a couple of milliseconds quicker than going through another route. This is an added refinement that can help get slightly better and faster fills, but it will take you time to learn which are the dominant ECNs for particular stocks.

Buy and sell orders

Don't wait until a potential trade is confirmed to set up your trade. Have an order entry window open for each setup you've identified. If you watch the pre-market, it's a great time to set up your orders for the open. (Most day traders don't trade pre-market or after hours; liquidity is lower then and trades involve more risk.)

Ensure you have entered your limit, the number of shares you are buying, and your preferred trade routing if you're using Level 2 (e.g. ARCA). If you have three or four windows prepared, you are ready to move as soon as one of your watchlist stocks hits the right price.

Hotkeys

If you use Windows, you probably know the emergency reboot command: alt + ctrl + delete. Instead of using a whole load of different commands, one combination of keys works to do the job. Similarly, you might use ctrl + B to make text bold, or ctrl + S to save a file.

The same idea of hotkeys applies in trading. You need to be able to trade fast. Let me talk you through the way I make an order with the broker that I use for my long-term investments.

• I search for the stock

• I select the stock

• I tick 'buy' or 'sell'

• I enter the number of shares I want to buy or sell

• I enter a limit price

• I check 'ok'

• I am then shown the trade and the commission, and asked to confirm the trade

• the trade is sent to the market and I wait a couple of minutes till my order is filled.

You can see the problem. While I'm doing all this, the market is moving, and I could miss the right entry point for my trade. More of a problem, if I have a stop-loss, or a profit target, I've got to go through that all again, and I may miss, particularly if I'm in a 'fast' trade like a momentum trade. I might hit an extra zero by mistake if I'm in a hurry. It's a slow and error-prone system.

That's why traders rely on hotkeys - shortcuts that let you trade quickly. And the best thing about hotkeys is that you can customize them yourself. Useful hotkey commands are:

• sell all my shares in this stock

• cancel all outstanding orders

• buy 100 shares, buy 150 shares

• reverse the position in this stock

• sell half my position - this is useful when you hit your first profit target and want to de-risk your trade

• set a new stop loss at the current price (or 11 cents below it, or whatever).

I should warn you, though; never use a wireless keyboard if you have hotkeys. Always use a keyboard hard-wired into your computer. Wireless keyboards are a liability; they run out of batteries, are slower than wired keyboards (every millisecond can count in day trading), and are susceptible to interference.

And once you've programmed your hotkeys, try them out in simulation first so you get used to them. You need to practice like a concert pianist to get muscle memory for when you really need to trade fast.

Watchlist and scanners

Finding the right trading opportunity is like looking for a needle in a haystack. With 3,300 stocks listed just on Nasdaq, if you just switch on your systems in the morning and start looking, you're probably going to find a good trade just as the market closes at day end. You need to have a watchlist of stocks that you trade, and you also need to have a scanner that will look for stocks that fit a number of criteria that qualify them as good trading potential.

Use the scanner in the morning to find stocks suitable for day trading - stocks that have gapped up or down, with high pre-market volumes, for instance. This will make up your watchlist.

When I am *investing*, I have a watchlist of stocks I'd like to buy but that are a bit too pricey right now. I check it every so often to see if any of those stocks have come down to the level that I want to buy at. But my *trading* watchlist is quite different. It's designed just for a single day's trading, and shows stocks that meet my criteria for "stocks in play" that will give me a good chance of a trade.

Get your watchlist made before market open, if you trade the open. Once you have your watchlist you can start thinking about what kind of trade each stock gives you the best chance at. For instance, if a stock is right at the top of its trading range, you're thinking about a range trade or maybe a breakout, or maybe a false breakout, giving you the chance to trade against it as the stock re-enters the range. If a stock gapped down overnight, a lot of market participants will be panicked into selling; there's a chance it will bounce up strongly once the selling pressure has faded away.

Having a watchlist filters out the noise of the 3,300 stocks all yelling their price tickers at you, and lets you concentrate on a select number of profit-making opportunities. And it helps your discipline, too.

Keep your scanner running during the day to catch new situations, maybe in reaction to news coming in. You might start with scanner recommendations from other traders, but eventually, you'll want to configure your scanner for the type of trades that 'click' with you. Everyone has their own personal favorite trade setups. Here are a couple of ideas:

• scanning for momentum - stocks with a high RSI (described later) plus high 15-minute volume, plus 52-week highs or lows

• scanning for reversals - stocks that are trading close to the outside of the Bollinger band, with very high or very low RSI, and at least four consecutive candlesticks of trend.

Fine-tuning your scanner settings will come with experience. It can be useful to look at your successful trades and see if they all have something in common that doesn't yet feature in your scan. Maybe you could add that, and see if you are getting more relevant ideas from the scanner and fewer flaky ones.

Community of traders

To be a good day trader, you'll need to be okay with solitude, and you'll need to motivate yourself. But that doesn't mean you need to be a complete loner, and in fact it's a great idea to find other traders to chat with.

Many traders are remarkably open to discussing their trades. But being part of the community isn't just about trading ideas. You'll also want to share things like which brokers you've found best, how to set up new hotkeys, everyday frustrations, and even how you relax or what breakfast sets you up best for trading.

You could look for day traders' groups on Meetup - there are two huge meetups in Chicago, for instance. Some major traders run open chat rooms where you can sit in on their trades and hear them explain their strategy. Some trade platforms and brokers have their own trading communities, and these can be worth your time getting to know. Check out whether they are moderated - ideally it's not a complete free-for-all.

Other trader communities such as Warrior Trading, Bear Bull Traders, and OneOption, are paid-for choices, and offer not just the chance to join the community, but also valuable educational materials and research services. Before you join a group, though, check out its reputation; some traders are honest and open, and genuinely interested in training other traders to do well, while others are more interested in selling you their view of the world.

Don't expect other traders to give you your trading system and ideas, though. Do your own thinking and evolve your own edge - and avoid groupthink!

Opening an account and placing an order

Opening an account is quite a paperwork-heavy transaction, particularly for day traders. Your broker or platform needs to know that you're a suitable person to day trade, not a deadbeat, and that you understand the level of risk you're taking on. It also needs to ensure that you're not money-laundering for a Russian oligarch or a drug baron, so it will want to know where your money comes from (e.g. savings, inheritance, bonus payment).

The paperwork is a pain, but you have to get it right. I have a directory on my laptop called 'credentials', and in it I store all the things that I get asked for by banks and brokers - a passport photo, payslip scans, a recent scan of my bank statement, and so on. Then I know how to get my hands on stuff quickly and the necessary paperwork becomes less of a pain.

Once the paperwork goes through you'll need to wire through an initial deposit (or send a check, but why pay the extra postage?). If you are planning to day trade, most stockbrokers will want at least $25,000 in the account, to meet the Pattern Day-Trading Rules. Of course, you don't have to trade all of it. When I started, 90% of the money in my account was long-term investments, and I day traded with the other 10%. Now my day-trading side has grown, I have a separate trading account.

Once the money is in your account, you're ready to trade… or are you? It's best to get well familiar with the system before you go live. Play with it a bit outside market hours and find your way around.

When you place an order, you run **execution risk.** That doesn't mean the firing squad, but what's called 'fat finger', for instance - adding a zero on the end that shouldn't be there. Or buying a stock and a call option instead of a stock and a put option. Or selling instead of buying (an easier mistake to make than it sounds). Or even, selling twice the stock you own because your finger hovered for a moment on the mouse. Practice making trades in real-time till you're super confident that you are not going to make those easy mistakes.

The gear you'll need

First of all you're going to need a good fast computer. This is not the time to install a lite version of Linux Mint on an ancient laptop to speed it up - it's time to get a new computer. You'll also want a second monitor or even a third. You can have your stock scanner on one screen, and your watchlist stock charts ticking away on another, so you can easily see everything you need and never miss the action in those stocks. Your scanner will let you catch any stocks coming into play during the trading session without losing your focus on your prime trading opportunities. It's just too easy to miss a move in a stock you're watching if you're having to tab between windows all the time.

You'll want to ensure you have a second Internet provider, as backup. Of course, this could mean a good mobile provider alongside your broadband provider, rather than a second load of broadband - but try to ensure your two providers are different in case one of them has network outages.

It's also a good idea to have a TV in your office, tuned to a business channel. Don't put it on too loud; you'll soon acquire the ability to tune into any mention of economic news or stocks, so you never miss a major news announcement.

Put some thought into where you put your office. It needs to be a place that keeps you in an alert and positive frame of mind. If you don't enjoy going into your office, you won't get great results. Ideally, you want natural light and plenty of it, but not in your eyes or on your screens - you may need to move things around a bit to get the ideal set-up. You want a chair that gives you good support or a standing desk if you like, and you need a good-sized surface for keeping your legal pad or log book.

Also, you need somewhere away from your keyboard to put your coffee. Don't ask me how I know that!

Day trading is your business: how to structure it

Set your business up like a business. How many trades will you make every day? What are you looking for as a trade setup? That is, what kind of situations are you going to trade? What is your risk-reward ratio? What win rate do you need to be profitable? You should have answers to all these questions as part of your business plan.

You should also know what hours you're working, what markets you will trade, and how you're going to keep records of your transactions. (The tax authorities will want them, but equally, you need to know how you're doing.)

Remember trading is your business. And you trade to make money. But you should focus on setting up and executing your trades efficiently, not on the amount you make. Your business plan may say that on average you'll be making $500 a day, but some days you'll be well up on that figure, other days you might have a losing streak. Don't get up in the morning saying "I want to make $500" or any other number, but "I'll spot at least three good trades and execute them perfectly."

After all, if you run a great restaurant, the aim is to make money. But you don't wake up in the morning and say, "I'll make $1,500 at lunchtime," you wake up and say, "I'll get the freshest fish and meat I can find on the market, and my sous-chefs and I are going to turn it into fantastically zingy Asian fusion food, and we're going to give our customers absolutely the best service." The money, if the business plan is a good one, will come along once you have a name for great food and great service.

Chapter 4 Quiz

1. Which of these do you *not* need from your broker?
   a) Margin
   b) A good trading platform
   c) A cup of tea and a biscuit
   d) Low trading costs

2. What is execution risk?
   a) When your broker might have you shot by the Mafia if you lose money
   b) The risk that a trade might lose money
   c) The risk that you will get your order wrong
   d) The risk that the market will drop while your order is being executed

3. What should your watchlist focus on?
   a) The S&P 500
   b) Stocks with high betas
   c) Stocks in an uptrend
   d) Stocks that suit your preferred kind of trade

4. Which of these do you *not* need to spend money on for your trading business?
   a) A super duper fast computer
   b) A good trading program (unless your broker has a good free one)
   c) Fast internet access
   d) Professional business cards

5. Which of these will your broker probably *not* ask you for when you open an account?
   a) ID
   b) Your bank statement
   c) Your degree certificate or professional qualification
   d) Where you got the funds from

5

Chapter 5: How to Find Stocks to Trade

I've already taken you through how to choose your trading assets. In this chapter, we will look at how to find the right stocks for trading on any given day. You are looking for the stocks that have particular reasons for making strong price moves, which are a good opportunity for you to trade. You'll perhaps end up with some 'regulars' that you enjoy trading and have a good feel for, but they may not always give you the trading opportunities you need.

Stocks in play

Stocks that are likely to see strong trading with good day trade opportunities are "stocks in play." There may be a number of reasons for that; for instance there might have been an earnings announcement, or a takeover in the sector which leads traders to assess the chances of this stock to be taken out.

You can tell a stock in play because it will be having a high volume day. If you see high volumes of trading in the pre-market, you can guess the stock is going to be a trading focus for the day, even if normally it doesn't move. You're looking for a high *relative* volume. For instance, Alphabet (Google) usually trades about 29 million shares a day on average. Your aim is to be trading in the stock on days where it's trading more than that - and you'll spot that if the pre-market seems to be unusually busy.

On a few days at the start of February 2024, Google traded over 50 million shares. The same sales volume occurred in late October 2023, and also late July 2023 and early May 2023.

The shares gapped up in early May and late July, starting an uptrend. In late October, they gapped down, then again in early February (see example on the next page). Financial reports often spark strong price action and high volumes. That's the reason strong price action and high volumes coincided in these cases.

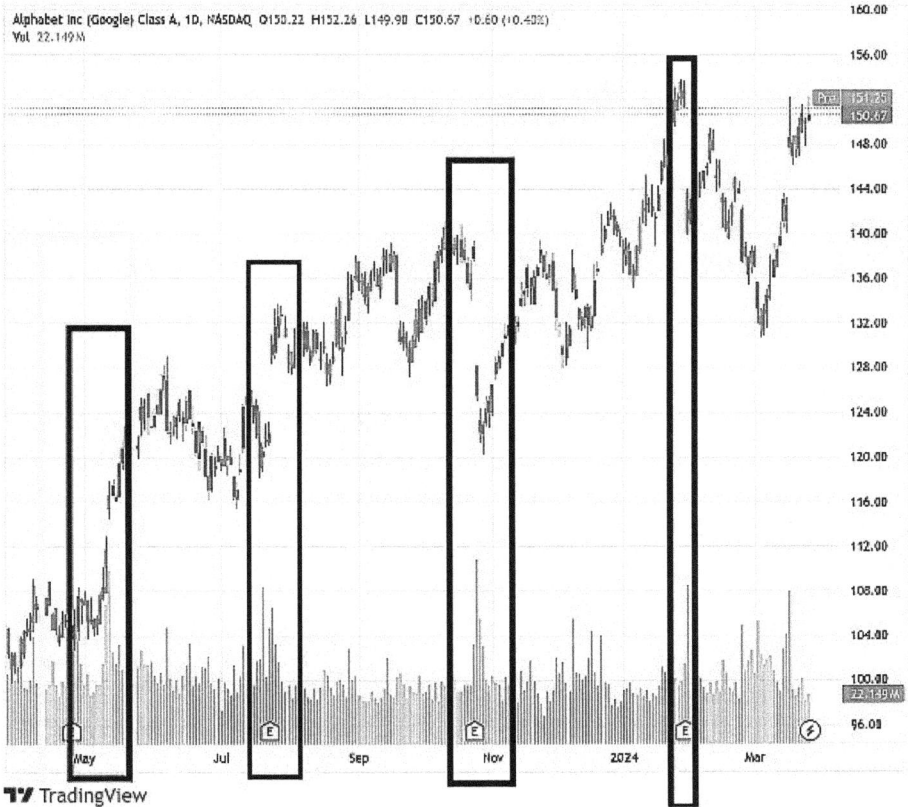

Fundamental catalysts for price action and trading volume include not just earnings reports and trading statements, but also results and profit warnings from competitors, FDA approval for drugs, large contract wins or losses, mergers, hostile bids, product releases, changes in top management, stock splits or buybacks, demergers and spinoffs. You may also see some stocks linked to commodities markets (e.g. oil stocks when the oil price moves significantly) or to particular countries (e.g. stocks with businesses in Russia) or to particular news (airlines, airports, and hotels during the Covid-19 pandemic).

There is plenty of opportunity around when there is fundamental news causing investors and traders to reassess the stock. Make sure you understand the basic news - 'right, it's a drug stock and its big drug just got approval', 'okay, it's a webstore provider and all its sites have been taken down by Anonymous'. You don't need to do any analysis or get stuck into the detail, but you know what's going on. If nothing *seems* to be happening to cause the price action, then someone else knows a lot more than you do (for instance, that a major investor is selling out), and you don't want to get caught.

Some traders hate stocks which are in the news cycle. They prefer to wait out big announcements for a couple of minutes before trading, or even not to trade stocks with results coming out at all. Me, I think these stocks give you opportunity, but you have to exercise discipline and wait a few minutes while everything shakes down and the price trends show up in the charts. Don't jump in feet first.

I also like to follow TICK and TRIN when I'm trading US markets. (Discount brokers often don't show these quotes, so I get them via my trading system.) These are indexes which show the number of stocks ticking up versus the number of stocks ticking down on NYSE and Nasdaq respectively. They are good temperature takers for the market. If they're headed upwards on a nice easy climb, I am happy with my long positions. If TICK climbs vertically upwards, I'm not happy because it's going to stall. Time to close out my longs, and go short.

On the other hand if both TICK and TRIN are looking poorly, in negative territory, I don't trade on the long side. It's very difficult for a stock to rise against a market that's got no confidence.

Float and market cap

To recap what I already said; you need to trade stocks that have adequate liquidity. But you also need to be sure the market in the stock isn't dominated by high-frequency traders. I look at two things: market capitalization and float.

Market capitalization (or 'market cap' for short) is the total size of the company's share value. It shows up on company data as one of the five or six major data points right at the top, and it represents the number of shares in issue multiplied by the share price. This shows the total size of the pool that day traders are fishing in.

Large-cap stocks are over $10bn market cap, and 'mega caps' are over $200bn. (Alphabet Class C shares have a market cap of $1.88 trillion.) Large-cap stocks have all the liquidity a trader needs, but the problem is that they are also the favorite stocks of high-frequency traders (a type of algorithmic trading). This means you're up against stiff competition from the automatic traders.

In the US, small cap means under $1bn in market cap, with a micro-cap at $50-250m. The smallest of these stocks are likely to be illiquid, making them difficult to trade, but above microcap status, you'll find that some small caps give very good opportunities indeed on the long side (they are still, in my view, not always liquid enough to go short).

Any stock with a market cap between $1bn and $10bn qualifies as a mid-cap. This is a good hunting ground for day trades.

However, as well as market cap, I look for *free float,* that is, the amount of the stock that is available to trade. For float, I'm not looking so much at dollar value as at the number of shares. For instance, a company with a market cap of $10bn but only two shares would not be tradable at all. And a company with a market cap of $10bn and 750 million shares in issue, but where the CEO owned 80% of the company, would also not be very tradable. At the very least, you'd be running the risk that the CEO buying or selling shares would have an undue influence on the share price.

On the other hand, Apple has a market cap of $2,865 billion, and 15.5 billion shares outstanding. Only 6% of those shares are held by insiders (who will probably hang on to their stock), so the vast majority of shares are tradable. Look further and you'll see that just over 50% is held by institutions, who are 'stickier' holders but may quite often adjust their positions in the stock, making lines of stock available to trade.

A good contrast is Value Line (VALU). It has only 9.6 million shares, which is a lot smaller than Apple's 15.5 billion. What's worse is that out of those 9.6 million shares, 91.62% are held by insiders. That means there are very few shares tradable on the market, and this, in turn, leads to poor liquidity, which makes Value Line very difficult to day trade as your trades may be badly executed or not executed at all. Value Line is both a small cap and a low float stock. I wouldn't touch it as a day trader.

Low float stocks that are a bit less extreme than Value Line do offer some good opportunities. They can move very, very fast, but they are tricky to trade; you may not get your order filled. As with small caps, they're only for trading long; shorting them is too risky. If you enter a short trade, you need to be able to exit if the price moves against you, but in low float stocks, you may find that there is not a market for your shares, and you can't exercise your stop loss. (Remember, the potential liability on a short trade is infinite - you can lose *more* than you put in.) The risk/reward ratio for a long position in low float stocks is high, and the best trade is a momentum trade - going with the flow. These can be profitable, but don't make them your main hunting ground.

Another thing you want to look at before you select a share for trading is the Average True Range (ATR). This tells you how much the share usually goes up or down every day. If a stock has an ATR of 25 cents, it's not going to make you much money - trading it would be like trying to train a hippopotamus to win the Kentucky Derby. You'll want to see at least 50 cents for a stock that trades at $50-100 a share, and if you see $1 or more, that's a good target share for day trades.

Pre-market gappers

Stocks that gap up or down in the pre-market - that is, the share price moves up or down in a single big jump, leaving a 'gap' on the chart - are always going to give you interesting trades. Often, they've gapped down because of news, perhaps bad results from a similar company in Europe announced overnight, poor trading from Asian and European markets, or trading news announced during the after-hours the day before. Analyst roundtables or recommendations can also have an impact on stock prices.

A stock screener can quickly find you all the stocks that gapped up or down more than a dollar in the pre-market. Make sure these are stocks that trade in large volume, so that you can trade them easily - over a million shares a day (Alphabet, with 29 million a day, certainly has enough volume going through). Look at the chart above and you can see clear white spaces before the stock gapped up - it's visually quite striking. This tells you there is a situation that might give you a good trading opportunity - but it hasn't created that opportunity yet.

Once you've checked the gappers out, you'll probably find that you can reduce the number of stocks you're going to follow intensively today to just four or five. You might just have two or three. That's fine, because you will get the best trades by really concentrating on just a handful of stocks.

I also like to look for 'follow-through stocks', that is, stocks that had a bull run yesterday and are following it in pre-market trading.

Real time intraday scans

Not all good trading stocks announce themselves in the pre-market. That's why you'll also want to monitor the market in real time. But again, you can't shift the whole haystack to look for your two or three needles; you'll need to have a real-time scanner working for you.

You're looking for shares that fit your other criteria and that have high relative volume today. That tells you there is something going on. In addition, you might look for shares gapping $1 or more during trading. You might want to look for stocks that are up or down more than 3-4%, which tells you there is something happening that's unusual and might give you a trading opportunity.

If you're using a momentum strategy, you'd set up a scanner to look for stocks with high relative volume and high activity in the last five minutes. This is particularly useful if you trade any low-float stocks, as momentum is really the only strategy you can make money out of with these stocks.

You may not need a scanner to get started, and since good scanners will cost you money in the form of a subscription fee, you'll want to be totally committed to trading and have some experience before you put your money down.

By the way, make sure you check for buy-outs and exclude them from your scan results. If, for instance, Warren Buffett decided to take his investment fund Berkshire Hathaway private at $425, it would gap up tomorrow morning from the current $398, but then it would never move again - it would just sit at $425 until it was delisted. (I have no idea whether this is a realistic scenario, but who knows?)

You might also want to check the sector charts. Sometimes, an entire sector, having been neglected for a long time, can become a focus of interest. You may find a lot of stocks in that sector have good trading potential. Commodity charts can show if a stock will benefit or suffer from a sudden change in commodity prices; if the oil price is going up, oil stocks are in play but so are airlines (their fuel costs will jump).

Some stocks have high short interest, and this is worth checking out. NYSE provides monthly short interest reports, which show how many traders have shorted the stock. (Warning: a monthly report is way out of date for a day trader, so don't put too much faith in it.) You may find that a particular analyst report or a particular investor has come out with a detailed argument for shorting the stock - this happened with two real estate investment trusts (REITs) in 2023, Medical Properties Trust (MPW) and Digital Realty (DLR).

Remember, you're not looking to take a view on the fundamental catalyst. It doesn't matter whether the earnings announcement is as good as it looks (analysts will always find something to complain about) because you're not trading on the basis of that announcement. Simply, the earnings release has put the stock into play and created price movement and good volumes of trade; but you will be trading on the basis of the chart patterns and your understanding of the market.

Chapter 5 Quiz

1. What's a good sign of a stock in play?
   a) It beat market expectations for its results
   b) It is trading in high volume
   c) It did not trade pre-market
   d) The company is sponsoring a football team

2. Which of these is not a fundamental catalyst for stock price movement?
   a) Company results
   b) Merger rumours
   c) A big analyst presentation
   d) Someone tweeted about it

3. What are TICK and TRIN?
   a) Two ways of measuring price
   b) Derivatives that track the NYSE and Nasdaq
   c) Stock tickers for Ticketmaster and Trinity Biotech
   d) The TV Hosts of The Great British Bake-Off

4. Why might big stocks not give you great trades?
   a) Their prices never move
   b) Their results are too predictable
   c) There are too many robot traders playing these stocks
   d) They are too difficult to trade

5. How do you trade a stock that's in play?
   a) By taking a view on the fundamentals
   b) By looking at brokers' advice
   c) By analysing the price charts
   d) By just tossing a coin

6

Chapter 6: Technical Analysis Made Simple

Stock cycles - how they help plan your trade

I already talked about how the stock market and other financial markets move in cycles. Stocks become "oversold" or "overbought," that is, the price has fallen so far there are no sellers left, or demand is no longer strong enough to sustain high prices; this results in peaks and troughs. These cycles are a result of crowd psychology, and can occur on a long or short timeframe; a commodities supercycle could take 20-30 years, but within that, there will be numerous much shorter cycles.

Traders use these cyclic patterns to predict what is going to happen to the price of the asset. Remember, markets don't move smoothly, they move in bursts. Imagine stretching an elastic band to shoot it at the wall; it will stretch farther and farther, then when you let go, it will whoosh away really fast. This is the kind of movement you're aiming to harness in your favor.

Technical analysis: picturing price

There are two kinds of analysis, fundamental and technical. Fundamental analysis for oil, for instance, would look at total production, total demand, and new exploration that might bring new oil fields onstream. For a stock, fundamental analysis will look at the underlying business and its management; earnings, dividend payments, news about new products, and so on.

Technical analysis, on the other hand, looks only at the price of a financial asset and the way that price moves. It considers price, time, and sentiment. Technical analysis uses charts to make clear the movement of price and other indicators such as volume.

Investors sometimes use technical analysis to find a good time to buy the shares in which they already have an interest. They use it 'cold' - looking at the pattern up to yesterday's close. They tend to use daily charts and look at a stock over a year or even five years.

But as a trader, you're using the chart 'hot' in real time; you're at the right-hand edge of the screen, looking at the chart unfolding minute by minute (or five minutes by five minutes) and waiting for one of the patterns that you recognize to show up before you initiate a trade.

Charting

Technical analysis involves studying charts of share price, volume, and other indicators to identify frequent patterns. You can expect these patterns to be repeated, as they reflect the psychology of market participants. A simple example: if the lowest a stock has fallen in the last five years is $57, then if it falls back to this level, then a lot of buyers will be tempted to make a prediction that it will not fall below it. They'll buy - and the stock will go up again. Market psychology means that to some extent, these charting patterns exist because people believe in them. If we all stopped believing in them, and all stopped using technical analysis, they wouldn't work anymore. But we believe in them - often subconsciously - and so they work!

Line charts are the most simple charts to use. They show the price on the y-axis and time on the x-axis, running towards the right-hand side. Remember, the right-hand side is where the future lies - that's where the trades are. Take a look at the example below.

By the way, when you see an explanation of a trade in a book or on a website, it's usually the whole chart you're shown, with the order entry halfway along and the way the trade played out all shown on the chart. You really need to cover up the right-hand side of the chart with a piece of paper and work out if you can see the pattern that led up to the decision to enter the trade. That's all you'll have to work on in real life.

OHLC charts give a bit more information; they show the open, high, low, and close for a given time period (a day, five minutes, one minute). Each time period is shown as a bar, with a line on the left showing the open and on the right showing the close. The length of the bar is extra information you didn't have on the line chart; it shows you the range of price during the time period shown (see example below).

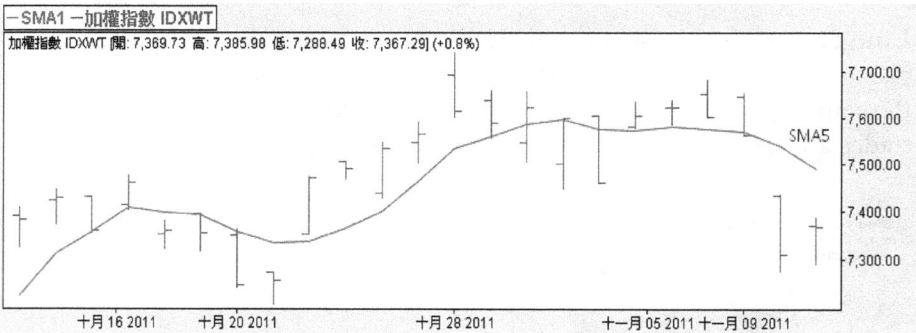

Then there are **candlestick charts,** which have the same four components as OHLC, but which many people find visually easier to use. (There will be a section specifically on candlesticks later in this chapter.) A colored and black & white example are shown below.

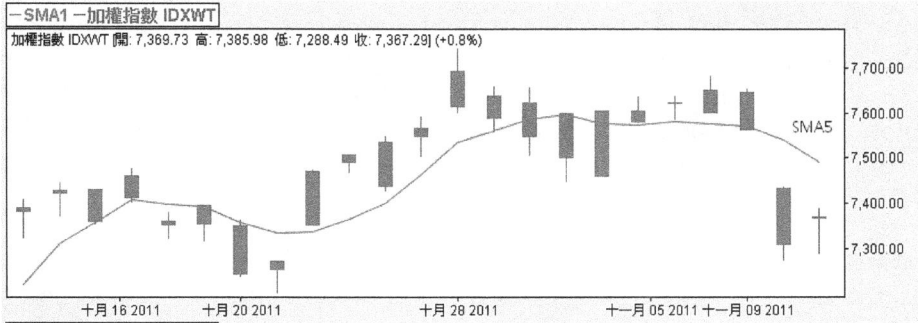

All of these charts can be plotted for any time frame. The usual charts you'll see in the media are daily, and they're intended for investors, but in trading we'll use much smaller time periods, like 15 minutes, 5 minutes, or just one minute.

But time isn't the only axis we can plot price changes against. **Tick charts** are not based on time; instead, the chart updates either on *every* trade, or on a given number of trades (for some reason, 233, 377 and 610 are popular). Otherwise, they usually look just like candlestick charts - just the candlestick represents a volume of trade rather than a number of minutes.

Range bar charts are also not time-based, but update every time a certain amount of price change has occurred; say, every penny that a stock price changes. The bar can remain open for hours, if the price doesn't change. For instance, you could use six ticks as a basis for charting S&P 500 futures. Every time the price rises or falls six ticks your chart will display a new bar. An example of a range bar chart is below.

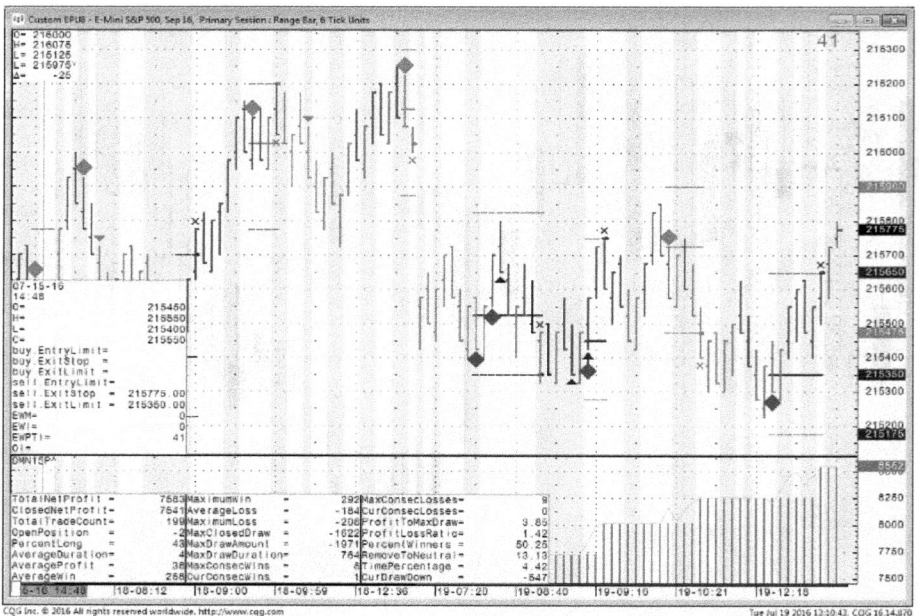

The **Renko chart** is just another way to show a range bar chart; it looks like a series of little bricks or tiles as shown below.

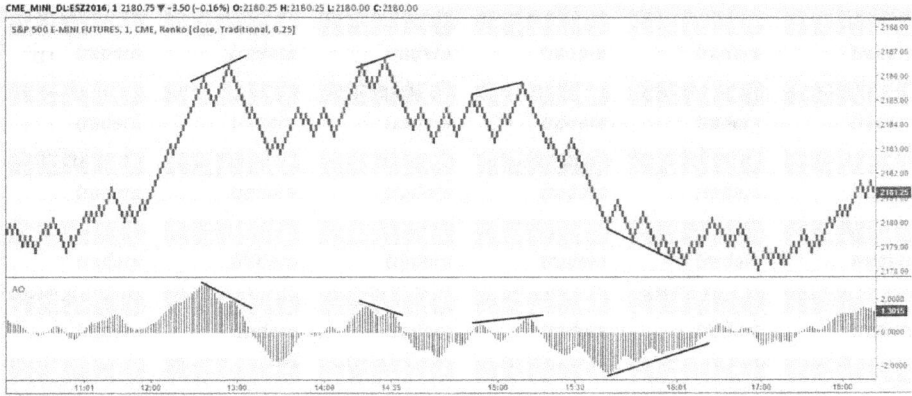

A *momentum* range bar chart provides an extra variation that is interesting; it updates when the price breaks *beyond* the range of the previous bar. This gives you, the trader, extra confirmation of the move. (You can easily spot the difference below - the range bars join up at their corners, the momentum bars have a gap between.)

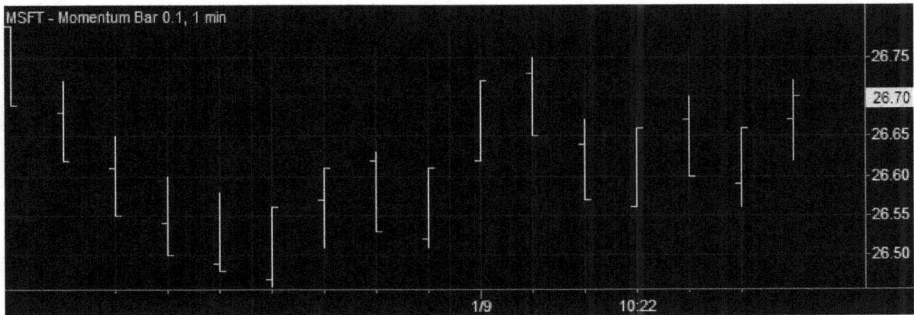

Support and resistance - what they are and how to recognize them

Support and resistance are two of the most basic concepts in technical analysis. Whenever you look at a chart the first thing to do is to identify support and resistance levels. The old way to do it was with a ruler on a paper print-out, but nowadays a lot of trading software will do it for you.

Here, you can see my handouts below, which may be familiar to the readers of the Technical Analysis for Beginners book! See how the share prices just touch the resistance and support lines. A channel has a resistance line at the top and a support level at the bottom - you can make some neat short-term trades inside a well-established channel, but the most profitable trades you'll make are on breakouts - which we'll talk about later in this chapter.

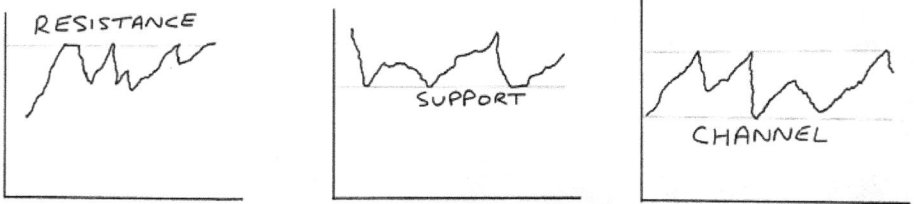

Supply and demand in the market are not price-agnostic. Market participants remember particular key levels, for instance, the price at which an IPO came to market, the lowest low that a stock has fallen to in the last year, or the price at which they bought the stock. That makes particular price levels significant and means that when the price arrives at that point, some of them will decide it's time to trade.

Sometimes, there are also fundamental reasons for a support or resistance line; for instance, a dividend-paying stock might rebound every time it comes to the price at which it yields twice the S&P average, and there might be resistance when it yields one and a half times the average.

Both support and resistance lines run horizontally across the chart. A support line is a floor; the price bounces back whenever it falls down to it. A resistance line is a kind of glass ceiling - the stock price can't get through it. Together, a support line and a resistance line can form a tight range within which the stock trades, and it takes a big push for the stock to break out of the range.

In the chart above, you can see a strong line at 173.40 which is a *resistance line* at the very start of the chart at 18:00, but later works as a support just after 19:00. The next line is at 173.88, and is close to another resistance line at 174.09.

If resistance is broken by a surge in the stock price, the resistance line doesn't disappear - it becomes a new support line. Each trading range is a new 'story' in the price house, so to speak.

The more times a stock tests a support or resistance line, the farther it's likely to go when it eventually breaks through. It's like bouncing up and down on a trampoline before you make a big jump and do a backflip.

Take some time to go on to TradingViews or another good site and use the 'horizontal line' tool to draw support and resistance lines till you feel happy that you're able to spot them.

Money making breakouts and breakdowns

Any time that a stock successfully pushes its way through a support or resistance line is called a breakout, or sometimes a breakdown if it's headed downwards. (Breakdowns are a good choice for short trades.) When a stock that has been in a pullback or a sideways move manages to break through resistance, it will generally move fast to achieve a new high. It will move fastest when there is a high volume behind the move. An example of a breakout, a false breakout and a breakdown are shown below.

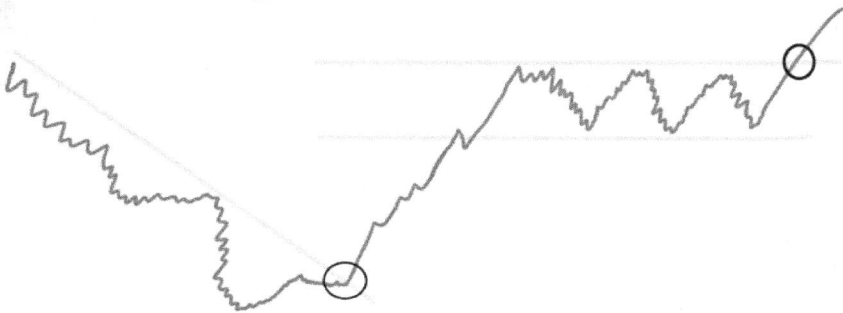

BREAKOUT

FAKEOUT
(JUST DIPS BELOW
TRENDLINE)

REAL
BREAK OUT

BREAKDOWN

Take a look at Levi's below. For the whole of March, $19 marked the top of its range. It couldn't break through. Then, on the 27th March, it broke through and raced up to $20, real fast. Turns out there was good earnings news in the pipeline - you can see the stock *gapped up* on the 4th April as earnings estimates were revised upwards.

I also took a look around this morning and the first chart I found that looked like a breakdown was Iron Mountain (see below). There's a downtrend for which I drew the top of the channel, then there are two support levels that formed, and then the stock breaks loose. Now, to be honest, I would have probably wanted to enter this trade a bit early, when it breaks through the $79.56 level just before 17:00. It wouldn't have hurt; as although the price tested that level a couple of times, it didn't break through. However, the real breakdown came at $79.44, half an hour later (just after 17:30) where a temporary support level had been established. I end up with a full dollar profit a share on that short trade which lasted for less than an hour.

There is likely, at some stage, to be a pullback towards the breakdown price. This gives day traders a second chance to go short again. In fact, because you have already had one iteration of the breakdown, entering at this point is a lower risk than entering on the first breakdown.

Shorting a stock is a trading strategy where a trader borrows shares of a stock and sells them on the open market at the current price, aiming to repurchase them later at a lower price. If the stock price *falls*, the trader can buy back the shares at the lower price, return them to the lender, and pocket the difference as profit. However, if the price *rises*, the trader faces potentially unlimited losses.

How to draw trendlines: just join the dots!

Charting can be difficult to get started in. Where an experienced trader sees price-making patterns, you just see them randomly crawling all over the chart. Learning to draw the trendlines will really help you understand the value of charting. Eventually, you won't even need to draw them - you will see them in your mind's eye.

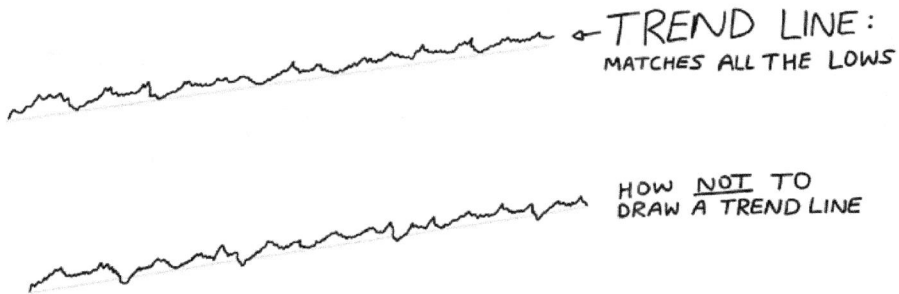

Trendlines aim to take the noise out of price movement. Instead of lots of tiny zig-zags, a trendline lets you see the stock's rate of ascent and descent much more clearly.

If the stock is going up, then it will do so in a number of jumps and pullbacks every time it hits a bottom and jumps again, this is one of the points you need to join fit a ruler to the bottoms - usually a clear line results, though they may not always fit exactly and there will be a few spikes outside. The better the fit, and the more times the price touches the trendline and remains within the trend, the better your trendline is as a prediction tool.

An example of how to draw the trendlines is shown below for Tesla.

Drawing both the top and bottom trendline shows the *channel* within which the stock is trading. When the channel is narrowing, there is likely to be a chance to trade on a breakout. In effect, trendlines act as support and resistance lines, too. When the stock price hits the top trendline, it's likely to pull down again, but if it breaks out, you could see a fast move upwards or downwards in the direction its headed in as you can see in the example below.

Technical indicators

Technical indicators go a little bit further than price charts. They carry out mathematical operations on the price and volume data in order to deliver more insight. For instance, the moving average aims to filter out the noise of the day-to-day price movements and give a clearer view of where the price is actually going. Technical indicators can tell you about momentum - the strength of a price move - and about oversold or overbought markets, where the balance has tipped too far to one side or the other.

The moving average is relatively easy to calculate, though you won't have to; every charting package will offer at least two or three moving averages. It's a simple concept; averaging the stock price across, say, a week or 20 days, so that you see a smoother line rather than the noisy jagged chart of single-day price closes.

The **SMA,** or Simple Moving Average, is the most basic of all these indicators. The 20-day is often very useful, while the 200-day SMA is a longer-run indicator that can show where the stock price is now in relation to its long-term trend. Add a medium-term average, like 50 days, and you have an interesting arsenal of different indicators.

The chart on the next page shows a 9-day simple moving average. There's no great trading idea here, but just take a look at how far the share price ranges from the blue moving average line, and when it follows it closely. One thing I find interesting is that there's nearly always a really large bullish or bearish candlestick when the price breaks through the moving average, which shows there needs to be a real big push for things to change. However, I don't think that has predictive value; you have to be very careful with moving averages as they are a lag indicator, that is, they tend to move *after* the price. You can't use them in isolation; they're most useful in giving you natural trendlines, and when used in combination to pick up changes in the trend.

Tesla, Inc., 2h, NASDAQ O174.14 H174.40 L173.33 C173.88 -0.27 (-0.16%)
Vol 777.262 K
SMA (9, close) 167.71

TradingView

Rather more advanced, the Exponential Moving Average, or **EMA** gives more weight to the most recent price data, and so it is likely to pick up changes of direction more quickly than the SMA.

A moving average can sometimes form a resistance or support line, which is very useful in confirming other chart patterns. Using 2 MAs together is also very powerful. When the shorter-term MA crosses over the longer-term line, it is often a sign of a powerful price move about to happen. If the short-term average moves higher, you have a 'golden cross', which suggests the price is about to explode upwards. Conversely, if the short-term average moves below the longer-term one, you have a 'death cross' which could signal a collapse in the price.

However, moving averages give a lot of false positives, so you need to keep tight stops if you're using them as a trading strategy, and use other indicators to confirm the signal before you trade.

Looking at the chart below, you get a couple of good golden crosses on 14 November and then again on 29 January (the green line crosses over the blue line), which would give you nice small profits on the remaining uptick. However, the apparent death cross in mid-December (the green line crosses under the blue line) is a lagging indicator, relating to the fact that the share gapped down. If you sold on this signal, you would have ended up in a stagnant or slightly rising share for nearly two weeks before the quick leg down.

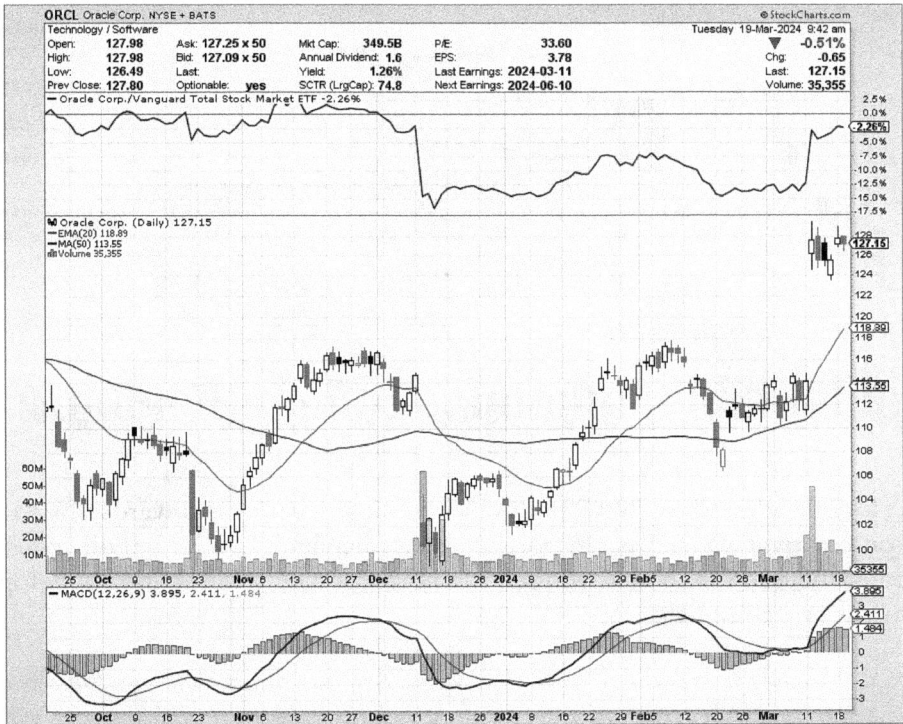

If you set up three or more different moving averages you will see a 'ribbon' which is quite interesting. When it tightens up with all the different averages coming closer together that often indicates a change of direction. When all the averages are running at the same angle in the same direction, that shows the trend has a lot of momentum behind it. Again, it's not best used as a signal for a trade, but as a confirmation if another chart pattern suggests a trade, or a sign that you might want to watch the candlestick chart for that stock quite closely today.

VWAP is the volume-weighted average price. This is like a moving average, but it includes the volume traded as well as the price in the equation. Because it includes volume, its relation to the stock price gives you a good feel for the balance of power in the market - whether bulls or bears are in charge. If the stock trades above VWAP, the buyers are winning. If the stock trades below VWAP, the bears are in control.

A lot of traders like VWAP trades. When the price moves towards VWAP, you can treat VWAP as a support or resistance line. In a long trade, you'll enter the trade as soon as you see a confirmation of VWAP, and your stop loss is any close below VWAP.

P.S. In Class 5 of the free bonus #1 companion masterclass, I demonstrate some practical ways of how you can use some of the indicators discussed in this chapter with real life chart examples. I would highly recommend you watch the free masterclass video after you finished reading this entire chapter by visiting: www.az-penn.com.

Momentum indicators

Momentum indicators are useful for judging the likely strength of a price movement.

Bollinger Bands (not named after the champagne, but after their inventor, John Bollinger) uses a moving average as the center, and shows the standard deviation of price movements as a ribbon on either side. That is, you can see both the average, and how much prices have diverged from the average over recent days. Most of the time, the price will move within the bands, and that can give you ideas for range trading - if the share price is close to the bottom of the band, it is likely to go back to the middle of the band, so it could be worth buying.

The width of the bands can also give you useful information. When they get closer together, it's as if they're winding up like a spring - this sets the scene for a big move in the price. If you look at the 'squeeze points' in the chart below (around December 10, and then around January 15) you can see how the biggest 'squeezes' are followed by big price rises that go as far as the top band before reversing.

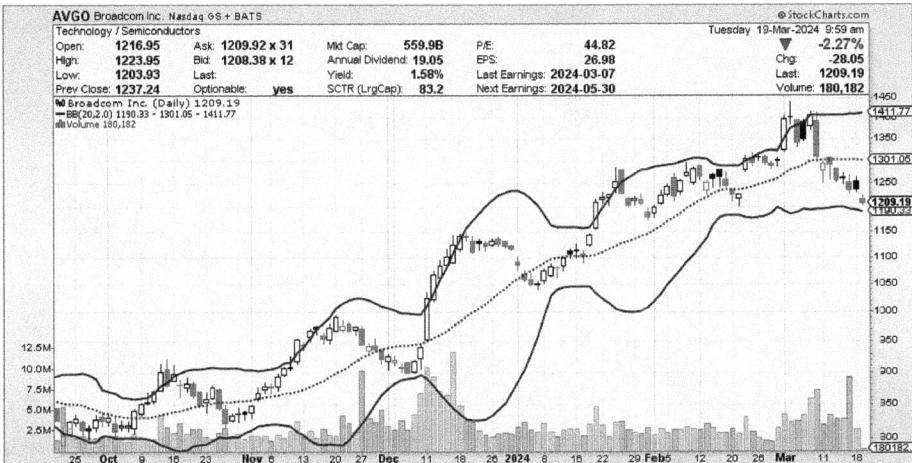

MACD (often pronounced 'Mack-Dee') is the Moving Average Convergence/Divergence indicator. It shows the relationship between different EMAs, and is usually shown at the bottom of the chart (sometimes on the chart itself) as two lines and a histogram.

Many traders use the 9, 12, and 26 time-period EMAs. In this case, the 'signal' line would be EMA 9, and the MACD line is the difference between the two other moving averages. Meanwhile, the histogram shows the difference between the 9-day average and the MACD line.

If the MACD line crosses the 9-day line, that often indicates the price is about to move in the direction of the cross. Most importantly, though, the histogram is there to be used as a check on the price information. If the price is hitting new highs, but the histogram is diverging, that suggests things could reverse quickly and the price could fall fast.

For instance, in the chart below, you can see how the MACD in the early part of the chart supports the price rises with notable peaks in early November and then again in December, but when the price rises in March, the MACD doesn't support it all, having very limited movement either side of its centre line.

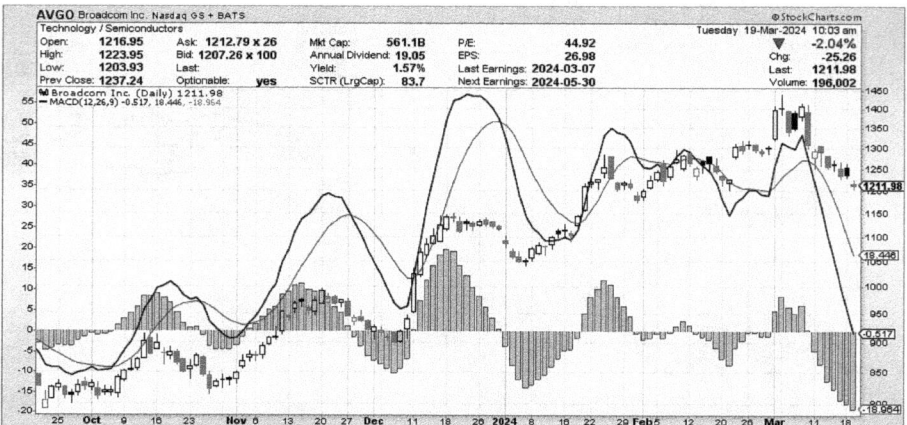

The Relative Strength Index, or **RSI**, is used to show how strong a trend is. It runs from 0 to 100, and often signals reversals if it's at the top and turns lower (or vice versa). RSI divergence from the price action, as with the MACD, suggests a reversal might be on the cards. You won't know for sure till you see the candlestick chart. A useful feature of many charts is that they will show an RSI higher than 70 or below 30 colored in, alerting you to an RSI that is likely to be a good price signal.

In the chart below for AVGO, you can see how the two colored sections of the RSI above 70 accompany sharp price rises in mid-December and late January. If you had bought the stock when the RSI had just got into this zone, you would have benefited from some fast price movement.

You may have spotted an issue with all of these indicators - they are lagging indicators. That's why they're only used to scan for possible trades, or to confirm trades, not to initiate trades.

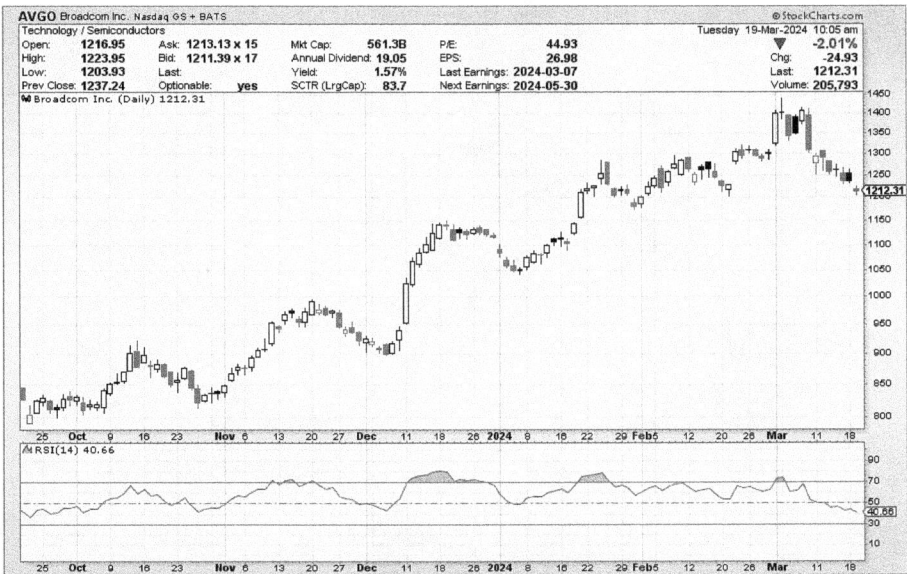

Oscillators

Oscillators will help you know if a market is overbought or oversold. One oscillator is the **Williams %R,** which looks similar to the RSI: it moves from 1 to 100 and shows the relationship between today's price and recent highs and lows. Below 20, the stock is oversold and could start to rise again, while above 80, it is overbought and is likely to fall.

In the chart below, DLR's price movements and the Williams %R are quite often related, but I don't see anywhere that I would have traded just on the basis of this indicator. However, in October, the stock formed a double bottom pattern, and if I had wanted to buy the stock at the bottom of the second part (right-hand side) of the 'W', I would have checked the Williams %R which showed oversold territory and that would have confirmed my choice of trade.

Stochastics are quite similar, though the math behind them is different. The stochastic oscillator compares the share price today to the share price history over time. The basic concept is that there's a certain average price progression, so if the stock has gone up very fast or down very fast, it has 'stretched the elastic', you might say, and will likely rebound in the short term.

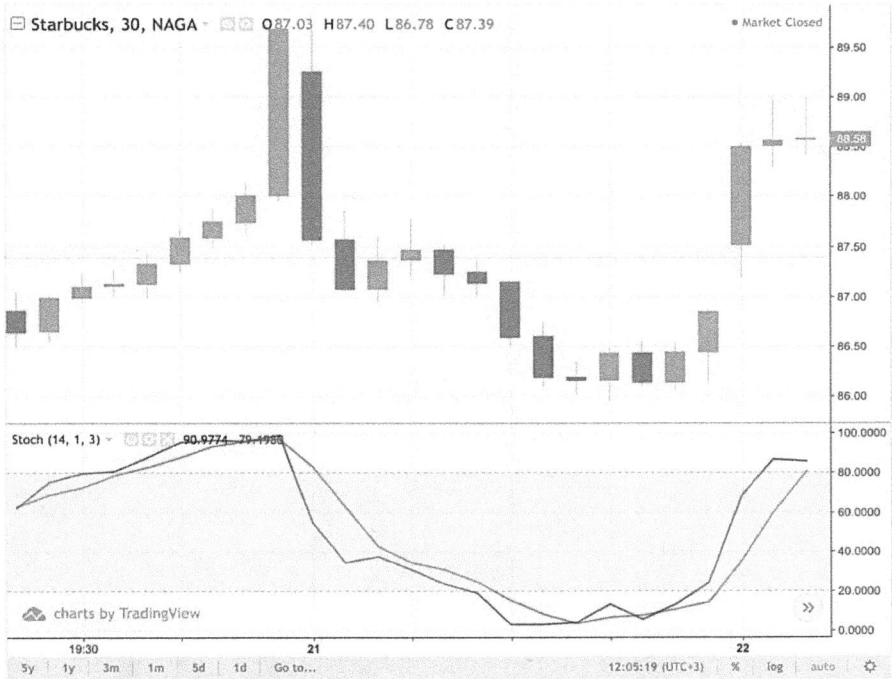

The stochastic oscillator is shown as a figure from 0 to 100. Under 20, the stock is probably oversold, and over 80, it is probably overbought. In this chart above, you can see how Starbucks was going parabolic (a very fast upwards curve) and at the same time the stochastic, at the bottom, crept over the 80% mark showing the stock was overbought. Trading short against the bullish trend might have been a good idea, but I might want to check some other indicators and perhaps have a look at a couple of different charts (a longer term chart for trend/support/resistance lines, or a different time period chart e.g. 1 minute instead of 5 minutes).

Oscillators are really useful if you range-trade. Suppose prices are at the bottom of the range and you want to take a long position to take advantage of an uptick, then if the stochastics show a value of 10, the market is oversold. That makes it a good time to buy into the trade. On the other hand, if the stochastics are still well above 50, that suggests you might want to sit this one out.

Before we move onto candlesticks, I would like to mention some good news. If you have enjoyed the topics of technical analysis, then I have an excellent book on Technical Analysis for Beginners by A.Z Penn which goes into more depth on this great subject. You might want to check it out!

Introduction to candlesticks

Believe it or not, the candlestick chart goes all the way back to seventeenth-century Japan, when rice traders invented a way of tracking the rice price. It's now most traders' charting method of choice, using one, five, or (sometimes) fifteen-minute candlesticks.

The candlestick is a box that is made up of the opening price and closing price for the period. If it closed up, the body is hollow (white); if it closed down on the period, the body is filled in solid (black). Sometimes, you'll see charts using green for upticks and red for downticks.

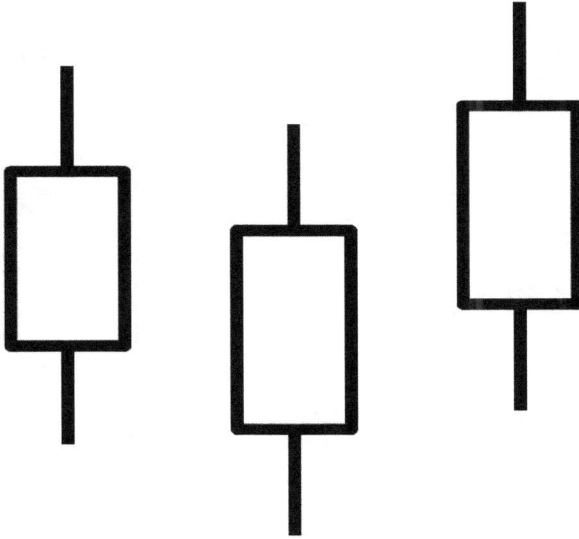

The highest price during the time period, if it is higher than the open/close, is shown as a line drawn sticking up above the box - the 'wick' of the candle. The low price, if it is lower than the open/close, may be shown by a line drawn hanging down below the box (a tail). The wick and tail are also often called 'shadows'.

Bullish and bearish candlesticks

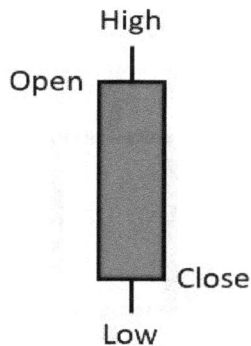

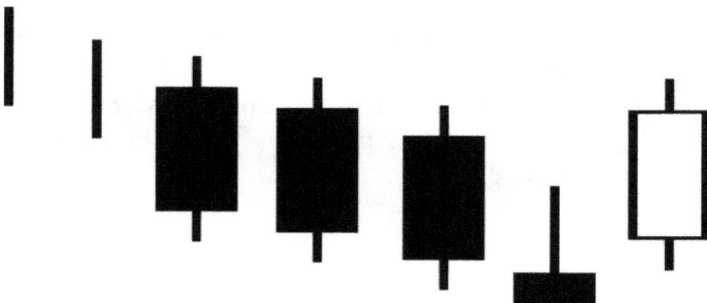

You'll often see a whole load of filled-in candlesticks in a downtrend. Conversely, uptrends often show white candlestick after white candlestick. The filled-in candlesticks show that for the given period, the price closed down; the white candlesticks show that for each given period, the price closed up. This is extra information that the line chart doesn't give you, and it enables you to see whether the buyers or sellers won the battle during that period. A white candlestick shows the buyers were winning - buying pressure sending the price up; a black candlestick shows the sellers were winning - selling pressure sending the price down. So a white (or green) candlestick is inherently bullish and a black (or red) one is naturally bearish. Examples are shown below.

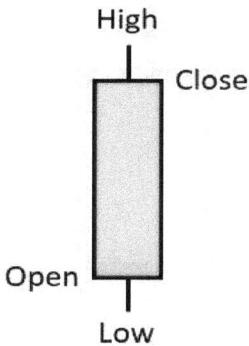

Bullish candlestick   Bearish candlestick

With any bullish or bearish candlestick, the larger the body, the more bullish or bearish it is. A very long 'pole' (or wick or tail) can confirm a reversal, and is often followed by another.

However, remember that when you're reading candlesticks you need to read the whole pattern, not just one candlestick.

Indecision candlesticks

When the market is indecisive, the share price will generally trade with only small variations from a flat line, and the candlesticks will bear this out. There's often a good spattering of both white and black candlesticks, and they will generally have tiny bodies and tiny wicks and tails, showing that the price has gone pretty much nowhere during the time period.

However, there's one candlestick that should make you sit up and take notice: the "spinning top." It has a tiny body, but it has a long wick and a long tail.

Spinning Tops

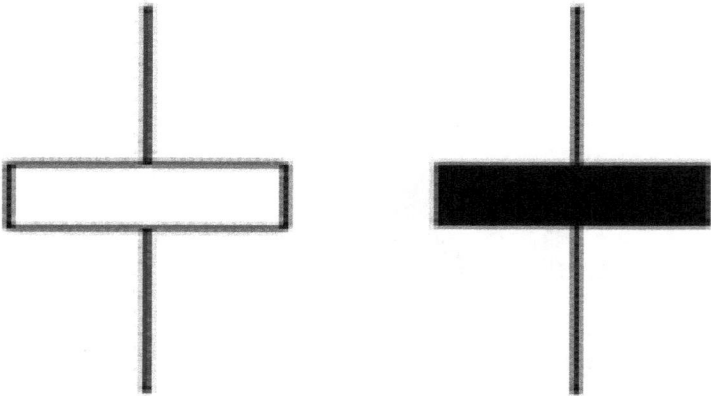

Let me talk you through what's happening in this candlestick. The share price opened, and then the bulls pushed the price up all the way up to the top of the wick, and the bears pushed the price all the way down to the bottom of the tail, but in the end neither of them won and the share price closed almost where it began. So, right now, the market is teetering on the edge, and it could take just a little push to move the price either way. That's why the spinning top is often the first signal that a reversal trend is about to start.

The spinning top will be the same color as the trend that is just about to be reversed. You trade in the *opposite* direction from a spinning top.

A special kind of spinning top is the **doji**. The doji is a spinning top that has almost no body. (In fact, the two spinning tops shown on the previous page are both dojis!) Often, the body is so small it looks like two lines crossing each other. When there is a very long tail on one side or the other, you have a very interesting doji, indeed.

The **hammer doji** looks like a hammer head on a long shank, and often tells you a bearish trend is going to reverse. The hammer doji's handle points downwards, in the direction of the old trend. What happened during the time period shown by a hammer doji is that the participants in the existing trend, the bears, pushed the price a long way in their direction; but by the close of the period, their opponents, the bulls or buyers, had pushed the price back to where it began. In other words, the tug-of-war was won by the bulls after a really hard struggle. That shows they are now in control, and the breakout is coming. An example of the hammer doji is below.

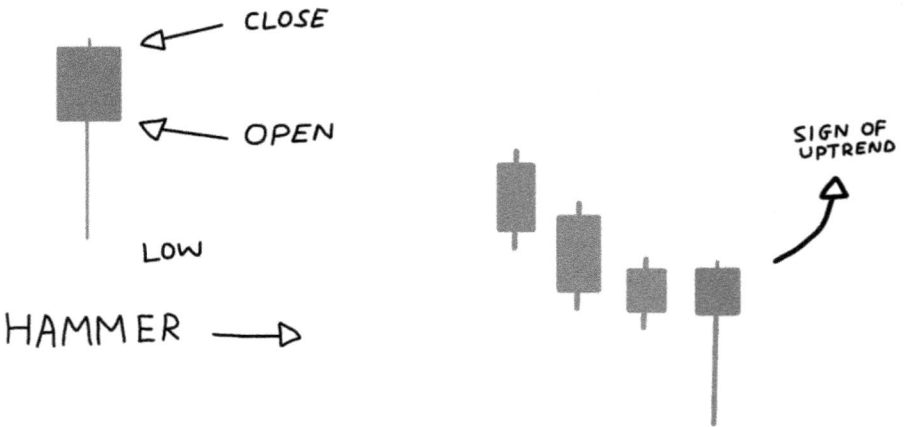

CLOSE

OPEN

LOW

SIGN OF
UPTREND

HAMMER ⟶

There is a very similar doji to the hammer doji that shows the end of an upwards trend. The only difference is that the handle of the hammer points upwards - it's usually called a **shooting star**, on the basis that it's a meteor falling to earth with its tail flaming out behind it. (But if you ask me, it's just a hammer the other way around.)

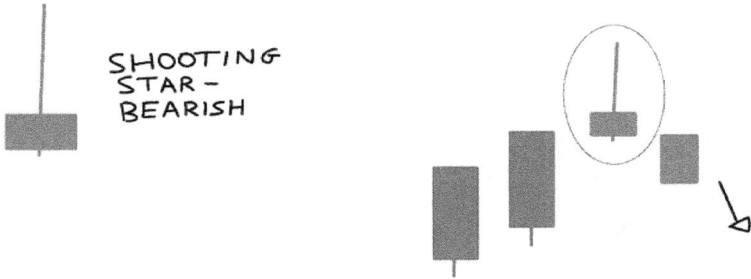

SHOOTING STAR - BEARISH

If you look at the Walmart chart below, just before 16:00, at the top of the last leg of the uptrend, there's a classic little shooting star, which I circled for you!

135

Candlestick patterns

The most important thing about candlesticks is learning to read patterns. If you don't, you'll make mistakes. For instance, the hammer doji works really well as an indication of the end of a bearish trend. But if you find the hammer at the end of a bullish trend, it won't help you. In fact, a lot of chart readers call it the 'hanging man' when it appears at the end of an uptrend, and see it as a bearish sign. It's the pattern leading up to it, not just the hammer doji, that's important.

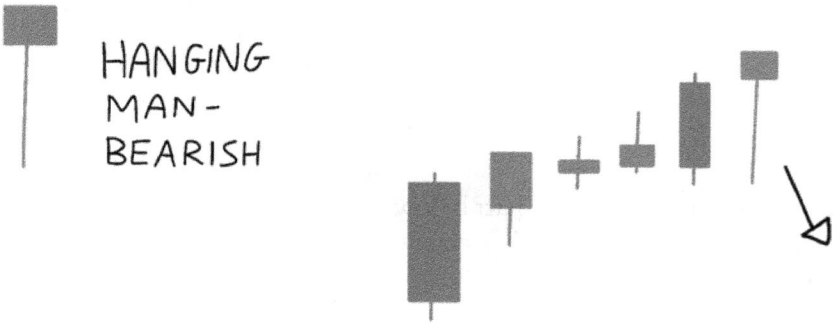

HANGING
MAN -
BEARISH

Top and bottom reversals

The nice thing about trading top and bottom reversals is that both your entry and exit points are very clearly defined.

If a stock is falling in the pre-market, it's really difficult to get in on the first trend of the morning - besides, you have no way of knowing how far it will go. But you can watch it for a reversal, and that's a good trade. At some point, you will see an indecision candle (a spinning top or a doji or hammer or shooting star), usually following a couple of very small-bodied candlesticks. This is where a reversal is likely.

To ensure that you don't buy into a continuation of the downtrend, you need to confirm two other indicators. First, the stock should be trading outside or close to the outside of the Bollinger Band, and secondly, its Relative Strength Index is extremely low. Then, your trade is set up, and you just need to wait for the first candle to make a new high. That shows you the doji was right - the trend is changing.

Buy at this point and at this price. Set your stop at the lowest low reached before the reversal. If the price falls, you're out. If the price trades sideways for more than a couple of minutes without reversing the trend, you should also exit. But if the price rises, stick with it and adjust your stop-loss upwards as you go. Your target is the next support level that you can clearly identify on the chart.

Only trade when the trend is strong - at least five, and better, nine or ten candles of trend followed by a doji or indecision candle. If the trend is not a strong one, the reversal (if there is any) won't likely be big enough to make you a profit.

Trend trading based on moving averages

Using moving averages together with candlesticks can give you new trading ideas based on trading with the trend.

For instance, when a rising trend falls back to the moving average line, and then follows it again upwards, you can trade that trend upwards. A 9 EMA is a good moving average trade, but you might find success with other moving averages (20, 50, or 200) - try them all while you are considering the trade.

Buy the trend at any point where the candlesticks *confirm* the moving average as support, and run the trade till a candlestick breaks the support line. Either use trailing stops, or monitor the trend and take some profit out once you have a winning trade, to reduce your risk.

So in the chart below, you can see how the price successfully tests the moving average line around January 20 but pulls away above it again after January 22, and then when a candlestick finally breaks down below the moving average support around February 13, it's time to exit the trade.

This could be a trade that takes some time, even two or three hours. The next trading setup, Bull flag momentum, is a much faster one.

Bull flag momentum

This is a very fast trade; you need to get in, grab the profit, and get yourself out again. So you probably want to wait to trade it till you are fully confident with slower and easier trades.

The chart for the Bull flag looks like a flag on a pole. A couple of big bullish candlesticks represent the 'pole', which is followed by a 'flag' flying out more or less horizontally with small candles. This 'flag' is the consolidation area.

Ideally, you're looking for a preceding upwards movement that was strong, with big bullish candlesticks, followed by much smaller bearish candlesticks. That shows the bulls have the upper hand, even though the stock price is taking a breather.

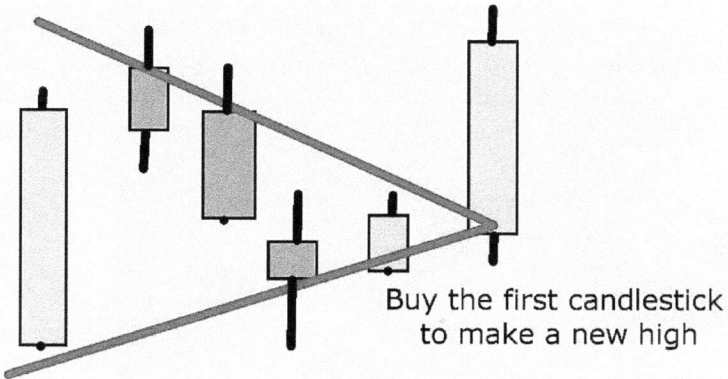

Buy the first candlestick
to make a new high

You start to buy as soon as the chart starts to show white (or green) candlesticks within the consolidation area. The stop-loss is the bottom *tail* in the consolidation area, that is, the lowest the stock has fallen during consolidation. (This is one reason using candlesticks rather than a line chart is really useful.)

One of the nice things about TradingView is that you can see other traders' ideas arranged under different headings. I checked the site this morning and someone in India had identified a nice bull flag pattern in BSE, the Bombay Stock Exchange index. A very strong move upwards, and a consolidation moving more or less horizontally and with very small candlesticks compared to the run-up. I might take another look at this one!

The trade setup works like this: you're looking at stocks that are headed upwards fast. You then want to see them trading sideways - not reversing the trend, but just flatlining or consolidating. So here in the chart below, BSE is a classic bull trend that ends up consolidating. At this point, you want to see either a horizontal 'flag' or a triangular 'pennant', and you want to draw in the lines that make up this flag (as shown with the red lines in the example on the previous page). Here, the bottom line is horizontal, but the top line is slowing downwards slightly. When you see a bullish candlestick break through your upper trendline, as it does with the very last candlestick here, it's time to execute your trade.

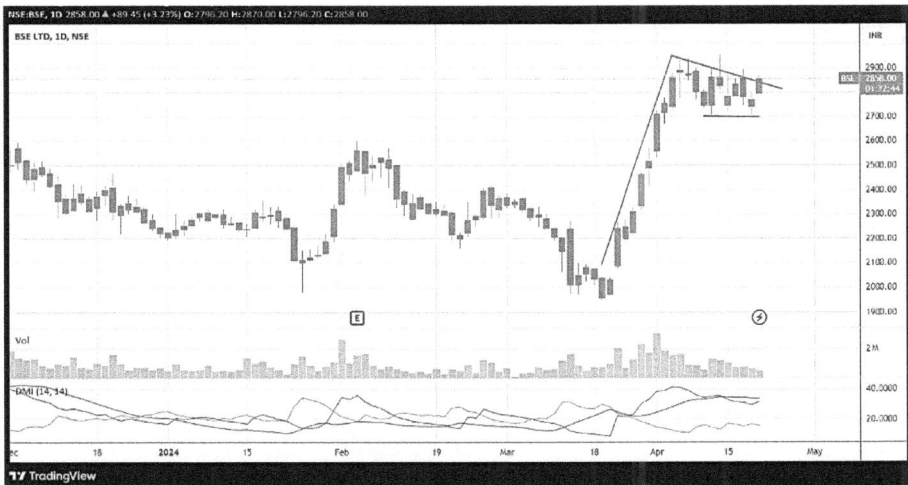

You might even get two bull flags, one after the other that you can make money out of. That's a great play. However, don't get suckered into a third one - it's usually flaky. Bull flag trades typically need to be played within a strong trend, in a small size, and fast.

By the way, if you're still unsure on bullish flag and pennants, I would definitely suggest you watch my free bonus #1 companion masterclass because in Class 3 I demonstrate examples of both patterns with real life charts – which will hopefully help your learning!

Chapter 6 Quiz

1. What makes stock charts work as a means of predicting price movement?
   a) The law of nature
   b) Market psychology
   c) Mathematical calculations
   d) Magic

2. Which of these are breakouts/breakdowns?
   a) The stock moves upwards through a resistance line
   b) The stock moves downwards through a support line
   c) The stock moves upwards through the top line of the trend channel
   d) The stock falls through the moving average line

3. What is a golden cross?
   a) The short term moving average moves up through the long term moving average
   b) The short term moving average crosses the share price
   c) The RSI moves higher than 80
   d) A bullish candlestick

4. In which of these cases would you want to trade on a price signal?
   a) Volume is abnormally low
   b) The RSI is trading in the middle of its range
   c) Volume is high with an RSI at the bottom of its range
   d) The moving averages are both going up

5. What is a doji?
   a) A candlestick with almost no body at all
   b) A bullish candlestick
   c) A bearish candlestick
   d) Somewhere that people study judo

7

Chapter 7: Planning Your Trades and Trading Your Plans

You won't get far writing a novel just sitting in front of a computer screen and a keyboard, waiting for inspiration. The same is true for trading; you can't just sit there and hope a profitable trade will appear, and you'll know what to do. You need to plan what kind of trades you're looking for, how much risk you'll take, and when to close the trade. Not planning properly is one of the most common ways beginner traders ruin their own performance, leading them to drop out of trading, often with significant losses.

Good traders make plans. They know what assets they want to trade, and what kind of trade they are looking for. They're willing to sit things out if they don't see a good trade today. It's the same with horse racing. I once went racing with a friend who was a big gambler. In a six-race card, he didn't bet on the first race. Or the second. Or the third. Or even the fourth. But on the fifth race, he checked the horses in the paddock, smiled, and went to place his bet. He'd chosen the one race which gave an attractive price on a good horse, he explained. He won - and chose not to bet in the remaining race.

What assets are you going to trade *today*? You might choose just one to concentrate on, or a number, but don't spread yourself too widely. Then think about how you're going to trade that asset; how much money you're going to commit to your trades, the level of risk you want to take, what events might have an effect on the market (including any announcements coming out today), the mood of the relevant market, what other traders might be doing.

You can now say whether on the whole you want to be long or short (whether you think the price of the asset is going up or down), whether you want to leverage, and what percentage of your total account size you want to use today. You also want to have a feel for your profit objectives and for how tightly you want to control losses. For instance:

• you might decide you want "risk two to get three"

• you know how many winning trades you have to make to reach your daily profit goal

• you know exactly when you will close out a losing trade (for "risk two to get three" as soon as your position is two ticks down on your buy price, for example).

Closing out your positions

How long does an investor hold an asset? As long as it takes. How long does a day trader hold an asset? No more than a day. Ever. It's in the name!

Day trading significantly reduces your risks. If you close your positions at market close, you have no risk during the hours the market is closed. If there is an earthquake in Japan, a profit warning from a stock in which you hold a position, or some other catastrophic event - you're not at risk. One of my friends swing traded a tech stock he was sure was on the rebound. One of its competitors in Taiwan came out with a profit warning while the US market was closed. It very nearly bankrupted him. If he'd been a day trader, he would have been fine.

It also reduces your costs, if you trade on margin. Overnight borrowing is expensive.

And it's a very good trade discipline. It stops you looking at a losing position and saying, "But maybe if I just hold it till tomorrow, it'll make money."

Don't believe the clichés

The markets are full of clichés. Many of them have some truth, but others are completely misleading. Take them all with a pinch of salt.

"Buy on rumor, sell on news." The grain of truth here is that markets are driven by expectation, so that a rumor will drive the price up in advance of the good news. Then, when the good news arrives, the market has already priced in (discounted) the information, so the price goes into reverse. However, not all rumors are based on fact, so you might be buying into a wild goose chase rather than a trading opportunity.

Also, markets often overreact to new information, so you might find 'wait for news, then exploit the overreaction' a good trading strategy instead.

"Cut your losses and run your profits." Or, as famed Fidelity fund manager Peter Lynch said, "Don't cut your flowers and water your weeds." That's a good motto for long-term investors, but maybe not so much for day traders. Remember, you need to track your value at risk as well as your profit on a position, so if you are ahead, but you now have a big proportion of your total value tied up in a single trade, it can make sense to close or at least reduce the position. With a lot of trades, you will have identified a target price based on the chart pattern; don't get greedy.

As for cutting losses, though - that is 100% right. Use stops and limits to ensure your losing positions don't keep losing you more money.

"The trend is your friend." Yes, some trades work best within a defined trend. But day traders work on a very short term basis. An investor might be interested in a long-term trend like the move to electric vehicles or sector rotation towards growth stocks. Day traders, not so much. The trends they care for are within-the-hour price trends. And sometimes your best available trade will be a reversal.

"The market is always right." Investors often don't believe this. They are looking for a good company they can buy cheaply because the market got it wrong. But as a trader, you should believe the market is always right. It will do what it will do. Your business is not to argue with it, but to jump on its back at the right point - and jump off again quickly if it starts running in the wrong direction.

"Pigs get fat, hogs get slaughtered." Take this one to heart; you should know the difference between aiming at a good profit, and getting greedy. If you start treating stocks like horses in a race and thinking that shouting at your trading screen can make them go up faster, you're leaving day trading for gambling territory - and getting greedy. However, I really love another phrase with pigs in: **"root hog or die"** - get rooting around for good trading opportunities, or you're never going to survive! In other words, *work hard*.

"Never catch a falling knife." If an asset's price is headed straight down, let it go. You run lower risks if you look for some stabilization or slowing down of the price declines before you buy into the trade. (Equally, never chase a stock that's going straight up.)

Setups and trading strategies

You can get all kinds of trading setups out of books or off the internet, but for the best returns you'll want to create your own, and then backtest them before you start trading.

Two basic types of trade that work well are breakouts and reversals. With breakouts, always trade in the direction of the breakout, and put a stop-loss just below the support level (for long trades) or just above resistance (for shorts). Prices may retrace to the support level several times before breaking out definitively, but if they fall below the support level, that's usually a sign that the breakout has failed.

Not to worry! Failed breakouts can also be a great opportunity. If the price looked like breaking out upwards, but the breakout failed, it's often a great time to open a short trade in the expectation that the price will fall fast back into the trading range.

Reversals can make great trading opportunities, but they are a higher risk than with-trend trades. Classic chart patterns like the double top or head and shoulders may show that a reversal is on the cards.

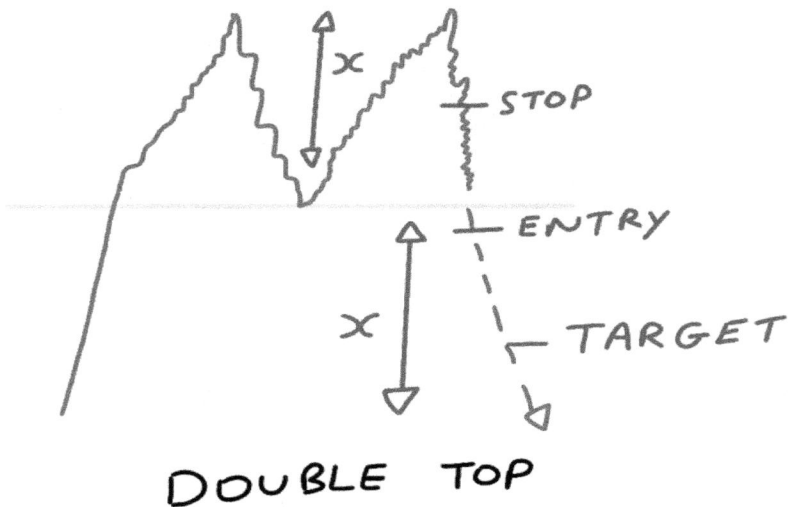

DOUBLE TOP

If you're in an in-trend trade and a reversal starts to occur, it can make sense to reverse your trade. For instance, a price might have broken out of its trading range and you've gone long. If you then see the price coming back to test the new support line a couple of times, it could be making a double top. It's time to close out your long position and maybe think about going short, to take advantage of a likely strong move back below support.

Pullback in a trend

Prices don't move smoothly. In any trend, there will be pullbacks. Even long-term investors know that you can take advantage of pullback to "buy on weakness" and lower the average in-price of your investment.

You're not looking for just any pullback, but for one where the price is coming close to a support level, or to a key price point or a moving average. That's a good time to buy, and wait for the uptick. You also know exactly where to put your stop-loss, and that's just below the support level or key price point.

However, pullbacks could be the start of a reversal. So take a look at the MACD for confirmation, and also take a look at a longer time frame chart to check there's no reversal building up.

Divergences

Divergences between the price action and technical indicators like the MACD or stochastics can signal a reversal. For instance, when a strong price uptrend is not reflected in the MACD, it could mean the bull move is running out of steam and prices could move strongly to the downside - a good time to place a short trade.

Check a divergence with the overall chart patterns before you decide to trade. This isn't a strong indicator on its own, but if it matches a pattern like a breakout or double top, you have confirmation of the trade idea. Examples of a positive and negative divergence are shown below.

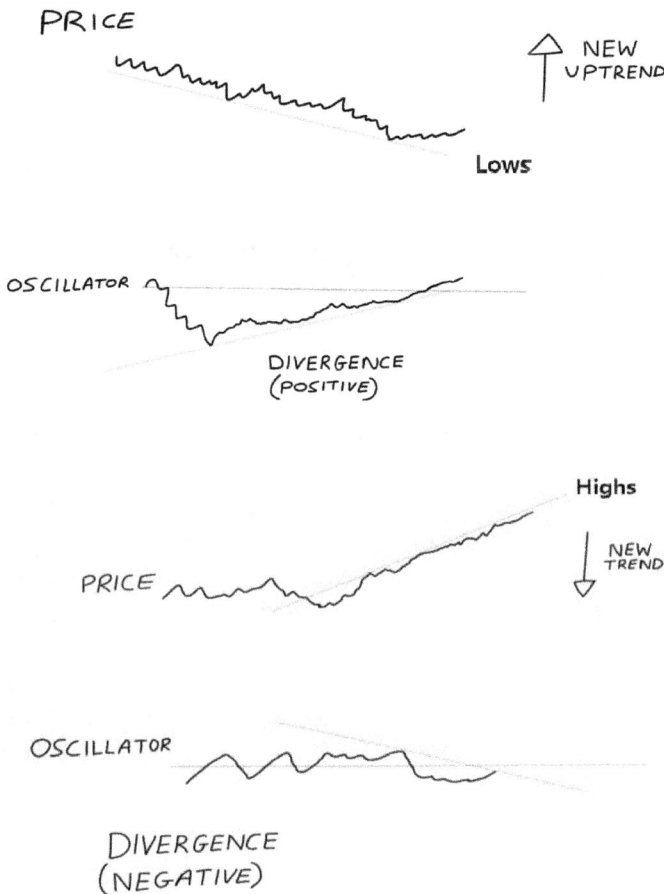

PRICE

NEW
UPTREND

Lows

OSCILLATOR

DIVERGENCE
(POSITIVE)

Highs

NEW
TREND

PRICE

OSCILLATOR

DIVERGENCE
(NEGATIVE)

Head and shoulders is a chart formation that has two 'shoulders' separated by a higher 'head'. It predicts a trend reversal, from the bullish trend that led up to the 'head', to a new bearish trend. If the right shoulder is weak, in other words, smaller than the left shoulder, that's a good sign there may be fast price action on the way down - the bulls haven't managed to push the price back up far enough.

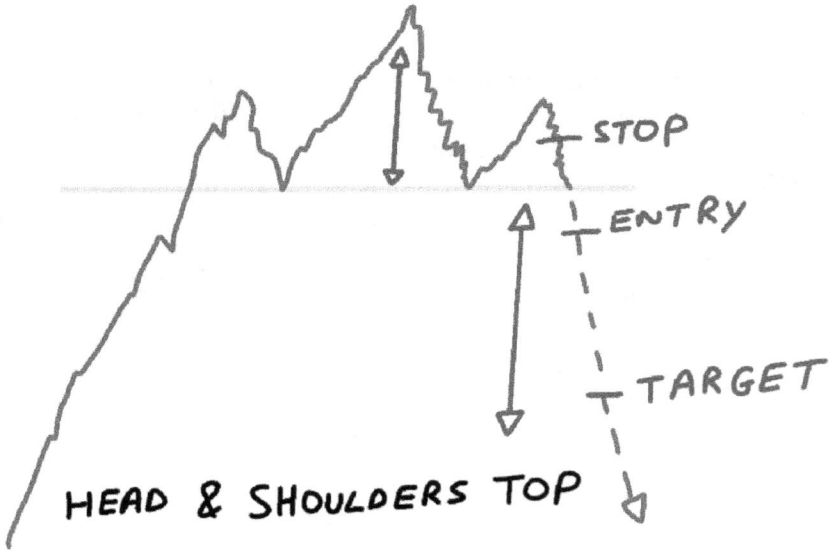

HEAD & SHOULDERS TOP

To plan the trade, you need to draw the support line, or 'neckline', that connects the two lows. You will then initiate a short position when the price dips below the neckline. The price target is equal to the difference between the lowest low and the highest high in the pattern (same as the distance between the top and the neckline), which becomes your target price fall from the neckline. You can create further targets at 1.5x and 2x the initial target, and take some profits or move your stop loss when the ce hits any of the target lines. This is a great system, because it prevents you closing your trade when there is still profit to be gained, but it limits your risk and with the 2x target as a hard limit, prevents you from getting greedy and following the trade too far.

The head and shoulders can also be inverted, in which case you would trade long, not short.

So, in the chart above, you can see how a head and shoulders pattern was established with a bottom at just over EUR 65 at around 13:30, and the neckline at EUR 65.10. So since that's a ten cents a share difference, I'm looking for roughly 10 cents a share downwards to my first target level, that is, EUR 64.90 (remember, we are shorting this position).

I'll go short as soon as the price breaks through the neckline convincingly, and it does, with a big bearish candlestick to give me confidence, just before 16:00.

On the other hand, I need a stop loss at EUR 65.10 because if the stock goes through that level, it will have destroyed the head-and-shoulders pattern, and all trades are off. Let's just put that stop-loss a couple of ticks higher, though, at EUR 65.12. That means I will only be stopped out if the pattern is decisively broken, and not if the price is just testing that EUR 65.10 resistance line.

That's my basic trade setup. However, I don't have to settle for ten cents a share, as head-and-shoulders formation often gives you a really good strong move that you can take more profit from.

One way to work these out is to look at further ten-cent declines - remember, that was the difference between the base and the neckline. So my next target would be EUR 64.80.

In that example, the stock nicely confirmed the pattern, and I would have exited my trade with a 20-cent-a-share profit, about 16:15.

Pullback setup

This is a low-risk, relatively high-reward trade that is quite easy to spot, so it's a good one for beginners.

A pullback in a rising trend (sometimes called a correction) will usually be followed by continuation of the rising trend. Learn to spot the end of the pullback, and you have a great opportunity to open a winning trade. To get this one right, look at the 20 and 200 moving averages. If the lively 20 picks up speed and starts chasing higher, it's a great indicator of a rising trend starting.

It's also worth noting that reaction moves like pullbacks often end when they touch the 20 MA. This is your hint for a profitable trade. An example of a pullback setup in action is on the next page.

Today, I saw Broadcom (AVGO) in a rising trend, as we see in the chart below. The blue trendline shows how the price was developing. There was then a pullback just *after* 19:00. The moving average didn't help me here, but based on the candlestick action I would have bought around $1324.50 just *before* 19:30. I might have sold out in the small pullback to $1328.64 that you can see just after that nice run of green candlesticks, and that would have made me around $4 a share profit in ten minutes or so.

However, at this point, I took a look at the moving average and saw that it had started moving up more markedly. That gave me the confidence to hang on for more. At $1337 or so (far right side of the chart), I would be out - the stock price has gone parabolic, which is never a good sign. The best profit is one you can take out in ready cash!

Look for the space

When the support and resistance lines are close together, trading is often choppy. But when there is a lot of space between them, the price will often move through the open space for a long time with no pullbacks. So look for the price moving into an open space, buy when it's a few ticks/pennies into the space, and sell five ticks/pennies later, or at least minimize your loss by selling half your position and letting the rest run. Some traders refer to these open spaces as "windows." Look to see how much room the stock has to run until it hits another support or resistance line - you may be lucky enough to hit a really good, long run.

You can also look at four lines on your chart to spot open space; previous open, previous close, previous high and previous low. Wherever the space is widest, that's where you'll get great trades.

However, you'll need to do some backtesting to find the right stop-loss position. You don't want to have a trade stopped out if there's just a little choppiness at the start, but you do want to get stopped out if the price starts heading in completely the wrong direction. You might also backtest whether adding second and third profit targets, with trailing stop-losses, would increase your trading profit significantly.

Let's have a look at two stocks that behaved a little bit differently today. In the chart below, Tesla has lots of resistance/support lines all over the place which are close together. There's a lot of zigzagging going on. This might be quite difficult to trade as you can't see exactly where things are going, but it's not impossible.

On the other hand, Apple, as we see in the chart below, has just **two** main lines of resistance/support, farther apart, and there's relatively little zigzagging going as the price moves from one to the other. So, if you spot the share price breaking through one of the support/resistance lines, you can predict that it will probably go pretty fast towards the next line, "filling in the white space." That's always an indication that you might be able to get some highly profitable trades out of the stock.

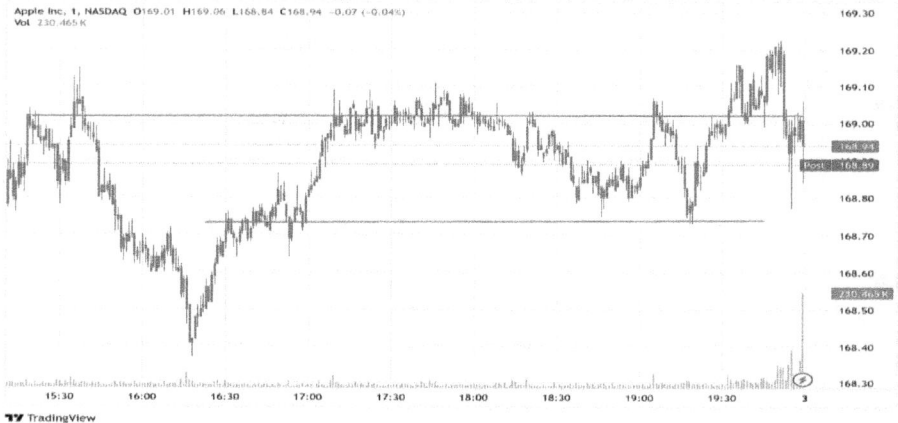

Keep looking

Sometimes, you will miss a first chance at a trade. Don't give up! Sometimes, you'll get a second chance. For instance, the price won't break out where your first chance happened, but will retest the support line. That's your second chance. Other times, you'll have a short trade planned and miss it, but if you stay around, you may see the price breaking out upwards, giving you a second chance to trade - though in the opposite direction.

Trade Execution

You could be the world's best reader of candlestick charts, but if you don't manage to place your trades correctly and get them filled by your broker, it won't do you much good. Flawless trade execution is important, and it's much more complex than just saying 'buy' or 'sell.' You need to know about different types of orders, and how to stack up automated series of orders to minimize the amount of work you have to do (and the chance of error).

An investor clicking the 'buy' button is usually making a **market order**. "I want 1,000 shares of IBM and I'll pay the market price, and I'll hold on to them until I change my mind." That's a bit vague for a trader, so you'll want to use orders that bring a bit more control. The risk with a market order is that you'll get your stock, but you may pay ten cents a share more than you were expecting. That could dramatically alter the risk/reward profile of your trade. To control that risk, you'll want to use a limit order.

The place for market orders is if you need to exit a position speedily. Say you went long of IBM at $183, but the stock started to fall rapidly and went through a key support level. You need to be sure you get out of that stock. If it's starting a major downtrend, you do not want to be left in IBM because your trade wasn't filled. In this case, you risk using a market order to close the trade (and ensure that if you have a stop-loss order, it's canceled at the same time).

A **limit order** lets you specify price. "I want 1,000 shares of IBM, but I won't pay above $186 for them." IBM is currently trading at $186.34, so the market will need to dip for your order to be filled. But if it does, and you get your stock, you will have paid exactly what you intended.

It's sometimes smart to use a little offset - that is, to use a limit order just a few cents higher than your intended buy price. For instance, I want to buy a stock at $55, but the stock might go through $55 fast, and my order won't be filled or might only be partially filled. So, instead, I'll use an offset and put in a limit order of $55.40 or $55.60 (avoiding the fifty-cent price, which is likely to be a key level for some traders), which will still get me into the stock around the right price. Most likely, part of my order will be filled at $55 and the rest at the slightly higher price. (Don't use an offset of more than 5% or so, though, or you're going to wreck your trades with slippage.)

A **stop order** also specifies a price - a trigger price for the order. For instance, if you have spotted a potential breakout but don't want to buy until the price has moved up to $186.50, you can say, "I'll buy IBM when it hits $186.50." That's a market stop. You can also make a stop-limit order, which also says, "I'll buy IBM when it hits $186.50 *and at that* price." If you're trading IBM and the market is not racing too fast, you'll probably get filled - but there is no guarantee.

Stop-limit orders are a good way to enter trades, since they partly automate your trade and mean you won't miss it because your attention wandered for a moment or you were occupied with another trade. You also won't enter your trade at far too high a price because the share price roared through the $186.50 level and your order was filled further up the spike.

However, stop-limit orders are not a good way to stop out a trade. Use a stop-market order instead for your stop-loss. Having bought your IBM at $186.50 with a limit order, you want to add a stop order to sell it if the price goes below the support level at $185. This limits the risk on your deal.

Why don't you use a stop-limit order? The answer is quite simple - if things go wrong, the price could move all the way past your stop-limit price without your order being filled. You would then not only have failed to control your downside risk, you would be incurring more and more losses by the second.

Ideally, you should create a 'bracket' when you open the position, with a limit order to close the position at your intended profit level and a stop order to close if the position starts to make a loss.

A **trailing stop** locks in profit, since the stop-loss is automatically adjusted as your trade moves into profit. If I bought IBM at $186.50, with a $185 stop, the stock might go all the way to $190 and then fall back to $184 fast; my stop-loss would be effective, but I would have lost all my profit.

On the other hand, using a trailing stop, once IBM got to, say, $188, my stop-loss would adjust upwards to $187. At $190, the trailing stop loss would adjust to $188.50. So when the price subsequently fell, it would hit the trailing stop-loss, and I'd be out of my trade with a perfectly acceptable profit.

Trailing stops are so useful, I would make availability of trailing stops a criterion in my choice of broker and trading system.

As a day trader, you need to remember to close all your trades at the end of the day. But this, too, can be automated through an order type - **market-on-close**. Any open trade with this order will automatically be closed at the end of the day.

Two other order types that investors don't use, but that traders really need, are OSO and OCO - order-sends-order and order-cancels-order.

• **OSO** puts your stop-loss and target orders in as soon as you open your position. Your opening order 'sends' the stop-loss and target orders as soon as it is filled.

• **OCO** ties up the loose ends. If your stop-loss is activated, it will automatically cancel the target price sale order. If your target price sale order is activated, it will automatically cancel the stop-loss.

If you bracket your trade with target and stop-loss orders in this way, your entire trade has been programmed. You have simplified your job; it's simply to spot the right opportunities and define the levels of acceptable risk and return. All the watching-price-moves-and-yelling-down-telephones stuff has been taken out of the equation, so to speak.

Although you have automated a lot of the thinking and acting, you need to ensure everything goes through as intended and that you don't have any orders left open that should have been closed.

For instance, if your trade hits its target, take the time to verify that your closing trade has been done - otherwise, enter a market order to close (market out) and ensure any stop loss or target price limit orders have been canceled. You might also "market out" if your trade is just sticking a penny or two below your target price.

By the way, always put your stop-losses just the other side of a key level (e.g. a round price, or a support level). You want to stop out just the other side, so that you don't sell out when the key level is being tested, but only when it's been broken. For instance, if you're buying a stock and there is a support level at $125 - a round number - then put your stop loss at $124.70. That way, you will probably be stopped out only when the trade is going against you, not when the price falls back before finally being able to push upwards.

Plan your trade, then trade your plan

A lot of day traders start without any particular plan. They learn a bit about the market, and then they just jump in and start trading. Most of them probably end up in the 90 percent of traders who don't make it.

The best way to ensure you'll make money day trading is to ensure you have a plan. Even if you don't understand exactly why a certain strategy works, if you've backtested it, run a simulation, and found that it produces a profit, stick with it.

You need to create trading rules which will let you quickly scan for trading opportunities, assess and limit your risks, and removes "gut feeling" and emotion from the equation. In other words, you are controlling your trades, rather than the market controlling you.

You should think about setting rules not just for individual trades but for when and in which markets you trade. Rules might include

• "trade the first hour of the NYSE"

• "finish trading by 11 pm"

• "I can quit if I'm ahead by lunchtime"

• "I will quit if I lose more than $150"

• "I will not run more than three trades at a time"

• "I will not trade a stock the day of its results"

• or alternatively, "I will focus on stocks that overreact to their results, on the day of the results, or on the morning after"

• "I will only range trade"

• "I will not trade within the first five minutes after a news release"

- "I will never risk more than 10% of my capital on one trade"

- "I will always check the MACD or stochastics before I trade"

- "I won't trade days with major economic announcements"

- "I will trade only when I can see a risk-reward ratio of two to three."

But don't forget you need to test those rules before you apply them. And then you need to stick to them. You'll need rules for your trading strategies, such as "Always move the stop-loss once you have hit your price target, to minimize your risk."

It's useful to have a rule about your daily targets. How many trades should you be doing a day? When should you stop trading? For instance, you might decide to stop for the day if you have a positive result after three trades, or by lunchtime. Then you can go to the park, play soccer, make sushi rice, cuddle your kids, whatever. This may sound dumb, but it guarantees you have some downtime and it also keeps your mind in a positive attitude. A musician friend of mine practices for an hour, and then waits till he plays a piece really well to put his violin away for the day. It leaves him feeling like a great player, instead of someone who has to do scales and arpeggios and still plays wrong notes.

You might also decide to quit for the day if you're on a losing streak; decide how long that has to be for you to quit, maybe 10 losing trades, or just a dollar amount in losses. That stops you trading in a negative mindset or with the desperation to make back your losses - which can result in taking trades with a poor risk/reward ratio, and losing more. But instead of relaxing, do some thinking. Why didn't your plan work? Did you miss the right entry point and pay too much? Was there a confirmation check that you missed out before making the trades? Is there something wrong with the plan? Or were you just out of sync with the market, which does occasionally happen?

You need to have dynamic rules that can adjust to different market conditions. For instance, if a trading rule says, "Set your price target where you make a 2% profit," that's not a dynamic rule; if it says, "Your price target for trading a head and shoulders should be the same as the distance between the top and the neckline," then it automatically adjusts to the situation and is therefore a dynamic rule. A lot of the rules you hear, like "always take ten ticks out of the market" or "wait for the MACD to go below 20," are not dynamic, and they will prevent you from taking good trades that will make 9 ticks, or where the MACD has been falling but is at 21, not 19.

You also need three key rules that you will never break. These are:

Rule 1 - stick to the trading rules.

Rule 2 - stick to the trading rules.

Rule 3 - stick to the trading rules.

Another rule I have is that I keep a written record of every trade. It's a great help when my mind goes blank halfway through a trade! Some traders just use a yellow legal pad or a notebook; I've printed out a basic log so that I just need to tick some boxes and add some numbers. That cuts down on the amount of writing I have to do but also makes sure I don't forget anything.

You may need to refine your rules from time to time. Don't be too quick to do that - sometimes the market will be just wrong for your system for a while, but if you have a well-tested, working rule, don't change it just because you have a poor streak for a few days. However, if you find that applying your rules has stopped you out of trades that subsequently came good, or that your limit orders are frequently not filled, you might ask yourself what could you do differently. Is your stop-loss too tight, or should you adjust for key levels? Are you being too optimistic or too demanding about your entry prices?

Having rules - trading rules and business rules, and risk and cash management rules - is what distinguishes the successful trader from the rest. You identify the chart patterns you're going to trade. You determine what is an acceptable level of risk and return. You set your rules. You use limit orders and stop-losses to manage your risk. And if you do this, you are going to make money. That's why you are trading, after all.

And if you feel the need for some adrenaline in your life, don't try to get it out of trading. Trading is for making money: climbing walls and paint-gun ranges and fast cars are for adrenaline.

Trading in action

Let's go through a trade. I've been watching a stock and I've seen it make a double bottom, a formation like the first three lines of a 'W'. I expect it to bounce off the bottom and roar upwards. (Here, I'm taking a swing trade rather than a day trade, which took about a month to work out, but the patterns are similar for day trades.)

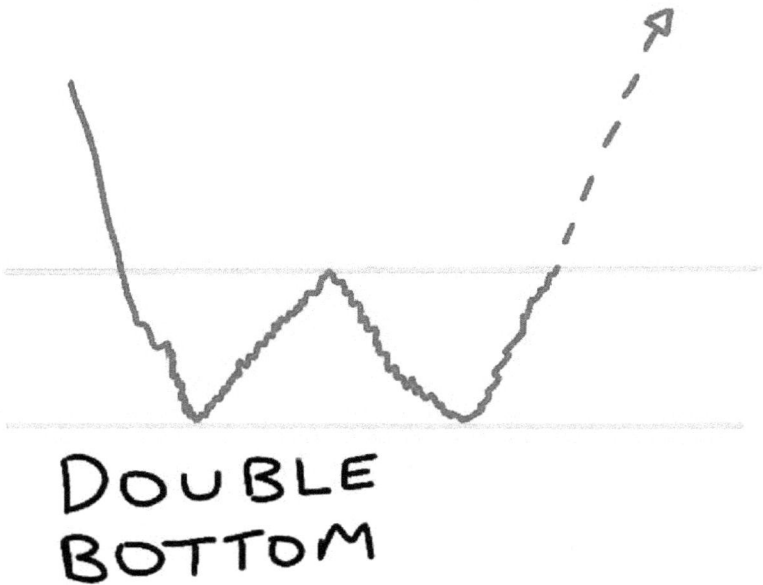

DOUBLE
BOTTOM

I first need to plan the trade. This means analyzing the chart patterns so that I can analyze expected profit levels and stop loss, and see if the trade fits my requirements for profitability.

So, 1) I'll go to the chart above and draw the support line for the 'W', that is, the line at the *bottom corners* of the W.

Then 2) I then draw the resistance line across the top of the *middle corner* of the W. Working from the patterns on the chart gives me everything that I need to know. My stop-loss will be just below the support line that we drew in the first step, and my initial target price is at the resistance line at $1.65. That would give me 20 cents a share in profit.

At 3) I can also see an interesting resistance/support level around $2, so I draw that in as my next profit target. I could also add another potential profit target at $2.40 based on the next resistance/support level, which you can see in a consolidation at the beginning of the chart, in October. There is a pretty clear gap up from $2 to the $2.40 level, so if the stock is running nicely, it's not likely to stop on the way up to that level.

If I didn't see these important levels quite clearly, I might just take the difference between $1.64 (at the top of the middle of the W) and $1.37 (at the bottom of the right side dip) - that is, my target profit. That's an expected 27 cents profit.

As a rule of thumb, once that profit target has been hit, the two further targets can be set at 1.5x and 2x the profit. That would give me $1.64 + ($0.27 x 1.5) = $2.04, and $1.64 + ($0.27 x 2) = $2.18.

When I hit my initial target, my plan is to sell half my position, then run the rest up to the next level, and I will also adjust the stop-loss to the previous target price, locking in my initial profit.

Now I have to decide how much to trade. That's easy since I personally have a 2% fixed-limit rule on my portfolio balance. That would be $500 on a $25,000 portfolio balance, for instance. And remember, this applies to only my risk on the trade (i.e. the amount I would lose if my stop loss were activated), not to the size of the trade I take.

I can now set up all the orders; a limit buy when the price bounces back off the bottom of the W, confirming the double bottom; a stop-loss; a stop-limit on half the position at the initial target price, and a stop-limit on the whole position at the next target price. All of that is entered, and so if the first order is triggered, my trade will play out automatically.

Step by step to a successful trade

Just to recap on everything you've learned in this chapter, let's go through a successful trade step by step.

First of all, you will have built your watchlist. You will just be watching a few stocks only, not the whole market. You'll have identified shares that offer interesting potential for a trade. So, among other opportunities, I am looking at a share that has been trading in a downwards trend today - Tesla - but the trend is slackening off. Will we see a reversal? In the chart below, at 13:30 (the extreme bottom left-hand side, which you can't see on the chart), the candlesticks are still bearish, but I can check some other indicators.

So at 13:35, while I'm waiting for a signal from the candlestick chart, I check the RSI for confirmation. The RSI is at 20 (the bottom line of the RSI part of the chart), suggesting this stock is oversold. I get a feeling that the bear trend could be running out of steam.

Remember, to succeed at trading, you need to make sure your preparation is perfect. You don't just see an opportunity and jump into it; you need to assess, for a given opportunity, exactly what you need to see in order to make a trade, whether that's increasing volume, the breaking of a resistance line, or a hammer doji, whatever. It's a lot of work, and sometimes the trade you're looking for never happens. But when it does, you'll be ready to go.

Now, here, I'd like to see declining volumes, too. However, in the chart below, when I added trading volumes, I see that they are still high, though not quite as high as 15 minutes ago (13:45 vs 13:30). So, I'll need to see a pretty clear signal from the candlesticks to be ready to trade.

A.Z Penn

Now, I work out, very quickly, where I need to put my price target and my stop loss. Is there a resistance level that will be retested if the stock starts to rise? I had a look at the earlier trading today which didn't really help, so I switch for a moment to the five-day chart, and there, I do find a level at $171 that looks like a good support/resistance level.

So $171 will be my price target - that's the place at which if the stock is going to fall back again, it will do so. In fact, I'll put my price target just *before* that, so that I will exit before anything nasty happens. If you hang on for every last penny, you're likely to find other traders exiting before you and the price falling before you can get out. As for my stop loss, I'll put that a couple of pennies below the consolidation point, when I see the consolidation in the candlestick, so if the stock heads downwards again, I'll be stopped out of the trade with only a small loss. But I won't know that till the actual trade is ready to go.

I also know the amount I can risk on this trade ($500, remember?). I have already got everything ready to go. I'm bracketing my buy order with two other orders, a stop-loss and a sell-limit order, so that all I need to do is hit the button when the price hits my target; which makes my job much simpler.

As I watch, by about 14:30, I see a spinning top appear. However, it's followed by a large bearish candlestick as the bears have one last go at driving the price down. Next comes a big bullish candlestick, and it's followed by another spinning top. I don't have what I really want, which is a hammer doji.

However, if I can get in at $168.50 at 14:00, put a stop loss at $167.50, and run the trade to $171, I'm risking $1 to win $2.50, which is a reasonable return. The RSI, together with the chart pattern, tells me I have a good chance of a reversal even though the hammer I wanted as conclusive evidence didn't appear. I place my trade.

The stock runs to $170.20 before encountering trouble about 14:30. If I get out after I see that big bearish candlestick, I will exit at $169 or so, so I've only made a 50-cent profit. But the stock rises to $170.90 at about 14:40 before the uptrend is definitively broken by a series of red-bodied indecision dojis.

No signal is faultless. The stock retraced nearly all its gains and didn't reach the $171 I expected. However, this was a *successful* trade. It was properly planned, executed, and under control. It didn't, as it turns out, make me much money, but I controlled the trade and didn't court undue risk by hanging on to the stock in hope.

Even if I had lost money, it would have been a successful trade because I am still solvent, still trading, and confident that my trading plan will work for me over the long haul.

In fact, as I'm still watching that previous chart, Tesla decides to give me a second bite at the cherry. By 14:30, the bear run is nearly over, as shown by a number of indecision dojis, and there are two bullish candlesticks, the second of which breaks out of the consolidation range. If I buy at $169.50, after that second green candlestick at around 14:35, I actually do get that run up to $171 that I was looking for, just before 14:45.

A final warning

Remember to always have a backup! So if your computer freezes, have a smartphone, or a broker you can phone. If you have a power outage, have a laptop with a fully charged battery and access to a mobile network while your wifi's not working.

You may even want to have two brokerage accounts... just in case.

P.S. Before we go onto Risk Management, if you are finding this book useful so far - I would really appreciate if you could spare 60 seconds and write a brief review on Amazon on how this book is helping you. It would mean the world to me to hear your feedback!

Chapter 7 Quiz

1. When should a day trader hold a stock overnight?
   a) When the position is losing money but it might turn around
   b) When the position is making money and will make even more tomorrow
   c) When the company has results tomorrow
   d) Never

2. Which of these gives you a good second chance if you missed the trade first time round?
   a) Bad results push the stock price back to its earlier price
   b) The stock retests the support line after an earlier move
   c) The RSI moves into overbought territory
   d) The price move falters on low volume

3. Which of these orders should you not use?
   a) Market-on-close
   b) OSO
   c) OCO
   d) Market order

4. Which of these is a good trading rule?
   a) I will take the afternoon off every Thursday
   b) I will never trade S&P 500 stocks
   c) I will always stick to the trading rules
   d) I will always make 2% profit on a trade

5. Which of these should you always have for a stock trade?
   a) A price target
   b) A stop loss
   c) A written record
   d) A good reason

8

Chapter 8: Managing Your Money and Your Positions

While making a successful trade is one of the things you need to be able to do, making a business out of day trading isn't just about trading. It's also about managing your account properly, in particular, managing risk. Failure to manage risk and to manage losses is one of the main reasons that beginner day traders drop out.

Risk and account management

You will lose some trades. By definition, you will make some losing trades. If you have a win rate of 93% (and that's really exceptional; you won't), you will still lose 7% of your trades. It's your job to ensure those trades do not lose big.

Look at the worrying arithmetic of loss: if you lose half your money, you will need to *double* your money to get back to where you were before. A 50% loss needs a 100% return to make it back. The odds are stacked against you whenever you make a big loss. (Which, incidentally, is why I am somewhat hesitant about trading leveraged ETFs.)

So, the first part of risk management is finding trades with a risk/reward ratio that will make you money. A lot of traders like to "risk two to make three." a 2:1 win/lose ratio.

If you buy 100 shares at $53 with a price target of $55, your risk if you just went long of the shares with no stop-loss would be $5,300 to make $200. That's a trade that is stacked against you. However, if you have a stop-loss at $52.20, your total risk has been limited to $0.80 a share, or $80 in total. You're risking $80 to win $200, which is a reasonable risk/reward level.

Of course, you'll need to make sure that you have correctly identified your profit target." I think it will go up" is not a reason to trade. "I think it will go up *till it hits the next resistance level at $55*" is a quantified and valid reason to trade.

Trades come along every day. Don't get FOMO and don't think you will never get another trade if you miss this one.

Trade management and position sizing

Your trading plan should include a clear statement of the maximum dollar risk you are prepared to accept. Say it's 2% of your portfolio; work out what that is first thing in the morning based on your total cash value. You might want to round it down or write it on a post-it note on your computer so you can remember it easily.

Let's see how many 100%-loss trades would be needed to wipe you out. If you risk 100% of your portfolio, that's easy: just one. If you risk 10% of your portfolio, that's ten. At a 5% position size, it would take 20 losing trades to wipe you out, and at 2%, 50 losing trades in a row. That's why it's a good idea to keep your position size low and never, ever bet the bank.

When you're looking at a trade, you need to estimate your risk per share, that is, the difference between your entry point and the stop loss price. Now, divide your total dollar risk by the risk per share, and you know how many shares you can buy. If I have a total cash value of $25,000, 2% of that is $500. So, looking at the trade I already mentioned, where my risk per share is $0.80, I said I was going to trade 100 shares. But in fact, with a $500 risk maximum, I can trade $500 / 0.80 = 625 shares.

I hate to tell you this, but you need to be able to do this calculation on the fly every time you are setting up a trade. I keep an old-fashioned electronic calculator so that I can do this without taking up real estate on my screens. A friend I know has a ready reckoner for various sizes of stop loss. Other traders do it by mental math. Work out how you're going to do it, and stick to your position sizes - this is what will stop you getting bankrupted by your bad trades.

Managing your money and positions is at the heart of becoming a successful trader in the long term. Every trader will strike a slightly different balance, but you need to be quite clear about the way you will manage your trades.

At the extremes;

• take too much risk, and you could end up bankrupt;

• take too little risk, and you won't make enough money to keep going as a trader.

Somewhere between these two extremes, you should be able to find your sweet spot.

First, find your **expectancy** - the return you expect to make. You'll need to test your trading system to do this, and you are looking for three figures;

• the percentage of winning to losing trades,

• the average percentage loss on losing trades, and

• the average percentage profit on winning trades.

You can then work out your average expected return on every trade. The math is simple: *(your percentage of losing trades x average loss) + (your percentage of winning trades x average profit)*. For example, let's say it comes out at 0.6%, then you'd expect to make 0.6% on every trade you make, on average, over time.

You can also work out your **probability of ruin.** That's a more scientific way of working out how bad a run of a few bad trades can be. Or rather, how bad does it need to be for you to be out of the game for good?

Take your advantage - the difference between your percentage of winning and losing trades. For instance, if you win 55% of the time and lose 45% of the time, your advantage is 10% (55% - 45%).

Then, work out the size of each position in terms of your total account value. Maybe you say you'll never risk more than 10% of your total - and you'll make 10 trades a day at that size. (Why 10? Because the math is easier to do, it's that simple. You might want to do 12 trades a day, or 20…)

Now work out the formula:

(1 - your advantage) / (1 + your advantage), to the power of your position size *divided by* your initial capital.

Yes, it's complicated. In fact, there are quite good tables that will show you the risk of ruin for given combinations of edge and position size.

Win rate	Probability of X consecutive losing trades within a 100 trade sequence									
	1	2	3	4	5	6	7	8	9	10
5%	100%	100%	100%	100%	100%	100%	100%	100%	100%	100%
10%	100%	100%	100%	100%	100%	100%	100%	100%	100%	100%
15%	100%	100%	100%	100%	100%	100%	100%	100%	100%	100%
20%	100%	100%	100%	100%	100%	100%	100%	100%	100%	100%
25%	100%	100%	100%	100%	100%	100%	100%	100%	100%	99%
30%	100%	100%	100%	100%	100%	100%	100%	100%	98%	93%
35%	100%	100%	100%	100%	100%	100%	99%	95%	85%	71%
40%	100%	100%	100%	100%	100%	99%	93%	79%	61%	42%
45%	100%	100%	100%	100%	99%	93%	76%	54%	35%	21%
50%	100%	100%	100%	100%	95%	78%	52%	31%	16%	9%
55%	100%	100%	100%	98%	83%	55%	30%	14%	7%	3%
60%	100%	100%	100%	92%	63%	32%	14%	6%	2%	1%
65%	100%	100%	99%	77%	40%	16%	6%	2%	1%	0%
70%	100%	100%	93%	55%	21%	7%	2%	1%	0%	0%
75%	100%	100%	79%	32%	9%	2%	1%	0%	0%	0%
80%	100%	98%	54%	14%	3%	1%	0%	0%	0%	0%
85%	100%	89%	28%	5%	1%	0%	0%	0%	0%	0%
90%	100%	63%	9%	1%	0%	0%	0%	0%	0%	0%
95%	99%	22%	1%	0%	0%	0%	0%	0%	0%	0%

Have a look at the table above to start your journey. To use the table, you need to know your win rate. Say you have a win rate of 70%, you would run down the left hand 'win rate' column till you get to the row marked 70%. Then, you can read across what is your probability of having a certain number of losing trades in a 100-trade sequence. With this 70% win rate, you actually have 0% chance of having 9 or 10 consecutive losing trades, and only a very small chance (2% and 1%) of 7 or 8 losing trades in a row. However, you would have a 100% chance of having 1 or 2 losing trades in a row though.

Or you can look at risk of ruin for your combination of stake size, win rate and return on your trades. This is a great dose of realism if you are prone to the error of believing that super-profitable trades will let you break even with a poor win rate. And many traders deceive themselves into believing that the next trade will be super profitable!

For instance, at a 10% stake size, the table on the next two pages shows that even with a really high rate of return on winning trades, if your *win ratio* is as low as 15%, you *will* be ruined if you risk a 10% stake size on each trade. (Certainty of ruin has all been highlighted in red. Just track across from 'win ratio 15%' and you will see every single box in the row shows 100% probability of loss.)

If you have a win rate of more than 70%, you do not have any chance at all of being ruined (the winning combinations are in green, indicating a 0% chance).

I suggest you view the table as traffic lights - red = stop trading, and green = carry on!

Win Ratio %	Profit is 1x your stake	Profit is 2x your stake	Profits is 3x your stake	Profit is 4x your stake	Profit is 5x your stake
Win Ratio 10%	100	100	100	100	100
Win Ratio 15%	100	100	100	100	100
Win Ratio 20%	100	100	100	100	46.6
Win Ratio 25%	100	100	100	30.5	16.3
Win Ratio 30%	100	100	27.7	10.2	6.1
Win Ratio 35%	100	60.9	8.2	3.53	2.33
Win Ratio 40%	100	14.2	2.5	1.24	0.888
Win Ratio 45%	100	3.41	0.761	0.426	0.329
Win Ratio 50%	100	0.813	0.226	0.141	0.116
Win Ratio 55%	13.4	0.187	0.0635	0.0438	0

Win Ratio 60%	1.73	0.0401	0	0	0
Win Ratio 65%	0.205	0	0	0	0
Win Ratio 70%	0	0	0	0	0
Win Ratio 75%	0	0	0	0	0
Win Ratio 80%	0	0	0	0	0
Win Ratio 85%	0	0	0	0	0
Win Ratio 90%	0	0	0	0	0

You'll also find a number of risk of ruin calculators on the internet. Those can be really helpful if you are not a math wizard. However, I'm going to take a look at the math to see how it works out. The math for a single trade if you have a 20% advantage, for instance, is: (1 - 0.2 / 1 + 0.2) = (0.8 / 1.2) = 66.67, or rounded to **67%**. (Because your position size is your entire capital, the fraction is 1, so that part of the equation makes no difference.)

On the next page, anyway, is a basic table where you can read off your risk of ruin quite easily. Find your **edge** in the first column downwards, then read across the top row to find your **stake size** as a percentage of your portfolio.

	100 %	50 %	33 %	25 %	20 %	16 %	14 %	12.5 %	11 %	10 %
2%	96	92	89	85	82	79	76	73	70	67
4%	92	85	79	73	67	62	57	53	49	45
6%	89	79	70	62	55	49	43	38	34	30
8%	85	73	62	53	45	38	33	28	24	20
10%	82	67	55	45	37	30	25	20	16	13
12%	79	62	49	38	30	24	18	15	11	9
14%	75	57	43	32	24	18	14	10	8	6
16%	72	52	38	27	20	14	10	8	5	4
18%	69	48	34	23	16	11	8	5	4	3
20%	67	44	30	20	13	9	6	4	3	2

If you risk your whole account on each trade, even with an advantage of 20% (60% win - 40% loss = *20%*), you still have a **67%** probability of ruin.

If you only risk 10% of your account on each trade, even if you have just a 2% advantage (51% - 49% = 2%, meaning that you win 51% of the time), you will have a **67%** probability of ruin than the trader with a 20% edge who risks it all, every time. Have a look at the table on the previous page and see for yourself!

This model assumes that you will lose 100% on all your losing trades, so it is actually a vast overestimate of your chances of bankruptcy. If you use stop losses systematically you should have much lower losses.

This model also assumes that you will put the same amount into every trade you make. In fact, money management should help you do better than the model suggests, and achieve higher returns than your expectancy indicates. A money management system aims to diversify your capital through a number of different trades, rather than betting the bank, and also aims to modify that amount proportionally to the level of volatility in your trading strategy. A good trading software or brokerage will give you an automatic money management calculator, so you don't have to do the math yourself.

Different types of money management system

There are various ways of managing your money. Some are simple, some are complicated, and some are downright dangerous. I have found fixed percentage works fine for me - it's easy to calculate and limits my exposure so that a few bad trades won't do me too much harm.

Fixed ten percent: this was adopted by WD Gann, writer of Wall Street Stock Selector and other texts on the market. It's a simple system, easy to calculate and use. You could use 5% or 2%, if you wanted. Personally, I think 2% is enough! With ten percent, you could lose quite a lot if you have a poor run of trades. However, critics of this system say that it's not very flexible, and it doesn't reflect market conditions.

Fixed-fractional: each trade is limited to a percentage of your account, adjusted for the risk of the trade (what you think you may lose). I dislike this because it lends itself to judgmental fix-ups - that is, you are at risk of infusing emotion into your trades. "I really need to win, so this has to be a low-risk trade, right?" No. Wrong!

The Martingale: doubling down. This money management technique comes to us from the world of the casino, where it improves the winnings from even-odds games like roulette. You start the day with a set amount. If you win, you trade again with the same amount. If you lose, you double the trade. But the problem with this is that it only takes a few losing trades to lose your entire bankroll. I absolutely do not recommend it for day traders. Also, while a casino might give you free drinks and food if you spend enough, the financial markets definitely won't.

The **Optimal-F** system developed by Ralph Vince takes a more sophisticated approach to past performance. It aims to increase your exposure in line with your edge in the market and the risk taken on each trade, as shown in your trading history. In other words, if you win 68% of the time, it will let you take more risk than if you only win 59% of your trades. However, it's a complex system to use - and of course, it won't work until you have a trading history to factor into the system. Most traders regard it as too theoretical for practical use.

The Kelly Criterion, or "edge divided by odds," aims to optimize your position size for your particular combination of winning trades percentage and advantage. However, it can be too aggressive - many traders use *half* the suggested Kelly amount, rather than the whole amount. Remember, too, that even the best traders have the occasional below-par day, in which case the Kelly system could lead to you losing more than with a fixed percentage system.

Protecting profits fixed-ratio system: this is used for trading options and futures, and it tries to balance your desire for exposure to the market with the desire to protect existing profits. The rather complicated formula was developed by options trader Ryan Jones, and it ratchets up the amount you should trade according to the amount of profit you have made *divided* by the amount you need to trade a second contract or lot of stock. This isn't worth it for beginners, but if you become a successful trader you might want to take a look at it to improve the efficiency of your use of capital.

Monte Carlo simulation. This advanced technique works by entering your risk and return requirements, and your account value, and running a software program which will tell you your optimal size of position. Where it scores over other ways of deciding the size of your stakes is that it adjusts to conditions in the market in a dynamic way. If you want to use the Monte Carlo simulation, you'll need to ensure you have access to the simulation package, either through your broker or with stand-alone software. It is *impossible* to calculate manually.

You will also need to think about what to do with your trading profits. If you are day trading as your full-time job, evidently you'll be using at least part of your profits as income to live on. But you might also decide to keep profits in your account, so that you can gradually increase the amount you trade. If you maintain your edge and your trading patterns, you'll then be able to increase your profits, too.

Another possibility is to skim off some trading profits from time to time, and put them into longer term assets. You might choose to keep a good slug of your money in low risk investments such as CD ladders, or to invest in stocks for long term capital growth. The return on these assets won't be as exciting as the return on your trading portfolio, but it should be more predictable, and take much less work. You can even set up an automatic plan with your brokerage firm to automatically move a percentage of your trading funds into another account every month or every quarter.

The principle of compounding

If you keep increasing the amount you trade in line with the increase in your cash available, the principle of compounding will come into play. Every time you increase your position size, if you keep the same win ratio and edge, you will increase your profits; and they will go back into your trading account where you can use them to make even more money.

However, there's one technique that seems superficially a bit like compounding, but is very dangerous. That's pyramiding - borrowing against your unrealized profits during the day. It can work, increasing your exposure in a rising market, but it increases your risk. If you use too much leverage and the market turns against you the whole house of cards can come tumbling down. Ensure, if you do use pyramiding - and it's a perfectly valid technique - that you have enough left to stay in the market even if your trades collapsed.

Managing the risks of day trading

Don't forget that besides the risks of day trading, you also run generic business risks and personal risks.

A major business risk is not having enough cash set aside to cover your taxes. It is a really good idea to set up a separate cash account and feed it as you go with your estimated tax on your profits. That way, you should always have enough, and if you've over-estimated, you can pay yourself a bonus.

You also need to ensure that you can keep control of your cash flow. This will need attention outside of trading hours. You will have subscriptions to pay, internet charges and office rent. Keep track of your expenses with a decent budgeting program.

There are also personal risks. It's very easy to get pulled into a negative spiral, getting addicted to the next trade (careful, you're not a gambler), or getting worried and anxious about the market. When your job takes over the rest of your life, 24/7, you need to worry. Being a good trader, you'll need to manage your emotions. Sometimes, the only way to do it is to lock the office up for the day and go to the park, or take a good long walk.

Sometimes, you can end up just feeling paralyzed, literally unable to hit your hotkeys. You can get overwhelmed. Learn to recognize that feeling, and don't trade while you're feeling that way. It usually means you've pushed outside your comfort zone by trying something new or scaling up your position size, so get back to basics, scale down your trades, and get your calm back before you re-enter the market. You need to be calm, you need to be focused, and you need to be in control of yourself.

Because you can't, ever, control the market.

Risk and fear in trading

Don't trade to make money; trade to *trade well*. Don't focus on the money, but on the perfect setup and execution of your trades. If you do this, and you have a good trading strategy, the money will look after itself.

When you begin trading, start small. When I began to drive, my father drove me to a block way out of town in an industrial area, on a Saturday, and got me to just drive around the block. In first gear. It took half an hour. Then we did it in second gear. Then we did it the next Saturday. There was no other traffic to bug me, so all I had to do was concentrate on starting, stopping, and making smooth gear changes. (Letting me drive an automatic would have been way too easy for my Dad. Manual stick shift was obligatory.) By the time I got on the road and had to look out for other traffic, I was pretty confident about the job of driving, and I could switch my attention to navigating multiple lanes safely.

So start with small trades. Start with just one trade at a time and just one strategy. Get used to that strategy. Get used to the speed of the market. Focus on a single time frame, too - don't chop and change between two-minute trades and longer-term trades. Sharpen your reflexes. Stay calm and focused. When you're ready, you can take on two trades at the same time, or use a new strategy. If you bite off more than you can chew, just clear your mind, and go back to what you were doing before.

Risk management

Some people will tell you "day trading is risky." (Remember that risk is something that needs to be quantified? So there is no such thing as "risky.")

In fact, every day trader decides their own preferred level of risk. You are the one who decides the risk-reward ratio for your trades. You are the one who decides how much value you will risk in each trade - two percent, or ten percent, say, of your total trading book. (I really do not advise 100%. You may not last very long as a trader with that strategy.) You also reduce your risk by not leaving any positions open overnight. You are only at risk when your positions are open.

If you simply buy 100 MSFT at $420, that's a $42,000 trade you are risking. However, if you put a stop loss at $415, you have limited your risk to $5 a share, or $500 in total ($5 x 100 shares). If you're expecting at least $7.50 in profit if the trade wins, that's $750 profit. You are risking $5 to get $7.50, or in other words "risking two to get three," which is a reasonably conservative measure of risk.

Chapter 8 Quiz

1. Which of these statements is true?
   a) You will lose some of your trades
   b) You will only lose trades if you take too much risk
   c) You must win more than 50% of your trades to make money
   d) You must have a 5:1 risk/reward ratio to make money

2. If you lose half your money on a trade, and reinvest what's left, how much do you need to make to get back to where you were before?
   a) You need to make 10%
   b) You need to make 50%
   c) You need to triple your money
   d) You need to double your money

3. If you buy 500 shares in Agglomerated Widgets for $10, with a stop loss of $9, your total risk is:
   a) $500
   b) $5,000
   c) $2,500
   d) Zero

4. What is the probability of ruin?
   a) Sixty percent
   b) The likelihood that a number of bad trades could bankrupt you
   c) Unlimited
   d) Another way of describing credit default

5. Which of these is not a money management system?
   a) Monte Carlo Simulation
   b) Kelly Criterion
   c) Martingale
   d) Vegas Twist

9

Chapter 9: Determining Your Profit and Your Profit Potential

Before you trade - testing your system

Even before you trade, you want to work out what profit your trading system *would have made* if you'd been using it for a while. You have identified the assets you want to trade, and the strategies you want to use. Now is the time to back-test them.

Even if you are using a system that someone else has created, it's important to backtest it. It might have worked ten years ago but isn't so good now, because markets have changed. For instance, there are more automatic trades going through - that has reduced the profitability of some types of trades. It might not work at all! Or it might work, but you need to assure yourself of that fact, and try to understand why and how the system works so that you know, when you get more experience, how you might refine it.

Even before back-testing, you can run a quick viability test. Look at yesterday's chart and see how many trades the system signaled. You might then look back a couple of weeks. Five or six trades is pretty reasonable. If it's only signaling one trade a day, it's not going to make you a living (at least, not on its own); and if it signals hundreds, you'll be run off your feet and probably end up making expensive mistakes.

You also need to check out the level of risk - that is, the difference between the entry price and the stop-loss, compared to the potential profit. Some traders' systems look great until you consider the risks they're running. If the system generates the right number of trades *and* it runs acceptable risks, then it's time to backtest it.

Backtesting uses software to run your strategy against historical price records for the assets you want to trade. You will have to be quite specific about your trading rules: "When I kind of think there's a bit of upwards momentum" *won't* work. "When a stock price in a downtrend reverses to move up by more than 0.5% with volume more than the normal level" *will* work and is the kind of strategy the computer can run for backtesting. Equally, "range trading big caps" is not quite specific enough; "buying AAPL when it hits a resistance level" is a better formulated strategy.

You may want to see what happens if you add more leverage, or make more but smaller trades. You may find that your strategy works with some stocks but not others: for instance, Tesla trades very differently from Microsoft, as it's more news-driven and volatile, so a range-trading strategy that works for Microsoft might not work for Tesla.

If your strategy doesn't work when you back-test it, think about why. You might need to refine the strategy; adding trading volume as well as price movement sometimes reduces the number of losing trades. You might add a tighter stop loss. Think about the idea behind your strategy; does the backtesting result mean that the idea is wrong, or have you missed out an important element of selection for your trades?

Most backtesting software can run an optimization program. This can suggest the best position size, holding period, and amount of leverage for your trading strategy. But be careful not to overcomplicate your strategy. Over-optimization is when you add so many variables that you're turning away profitable trades - it fits the historic data terrifically well, but what you've done is model a strategy that fits that data, rather than a strategy that will work in future as well. It's always difficult to know when you've moved from refining your strategy to over-optimization, but good traders and data analysts get a feel for it.

Remember to backtest your strategy to see how it does in different markets. A strategy that worked well in 2000 as the tech market boomed might not have worked in 2007 as the financial crisis hit. A strategy that works in range-bound markets may not work so well in more volatile markets. Consider periods of economic growth versus recession, high versus low inflation; does the strategy work for both?

Once you've backtested, it's time to start simulation - trading on paper, or 'ghost trading'. Use your strategy, but just write down your trades rather than actually doing them. Some brokers, like eToro and Interactive Brokers, provide simulation packages online, which cuts a lot of the paperwork out and feels more like real trading. Simulation will show you whether your ideas will work out, except for one small weakness; they can't show whether you would have been able to fill your orders. If you're trading small positions in mega cap stocks, probably this won't matter, but in some other markets it could mean your simulation will show better results than you'll get in reality.

Don't hurry this process. It could take you months to find the right strategy and refine it so that it works well. But this investment of time will pay dividends later. Skimp it, and you could get suboptimal returns, which is a nice way of saying you could lose a lot of money quite fast.

Tracking your trades

The simplest way of tracking your trades is simply to use a spreadsheet that shows the asset, date and time traded, price, quantity, and commission, together with the risk taken, and the same data for the close-out, with a final column showing your profit or loss and percentage return on the risk. Also, add a column with W or L for win or loss. This makes tracking your win/loss ratio easier. However, this can be cumbersome for frequent traders, so you might consider purpose made software such as Tradezella or TraderSync.

You also need to daily track your win/loss ratio and your trading profit as a percentage of your trading capital. This is your daily business dashboard. You can also convert your daily profit into "salary"; that is, trading profit divided by the hours you worked. (If it ends up less than $7.25, you're working for less than minimum wage at the moment. How do you feel about that?)

As well as just tracking the numbers, you need to track the qualitative side of your trades. Why did you make each trade? How did you feel about it - confident, or worried? Do you think you closed out too quickly, or not quickly enough? Were you following your system, or a hunch, or trading on news? Even if you're busy trading, scribble something down on a sheet of paper and look back at it at the end of the day before writing up your diary. Trade journaling software makes this part of the process easier.

Calculating overall performance

In an ideal world, you'd start with $25,000 say on January 1st, and you'd trade with that $25,000 all the way through to December 31st without taking any money out, or adding any extra capital, and calculating your annual performance would be real easy.

In fact, you're likely to have taken a bit out of the trading fund as downpayment on a new car, or added a bit when your tax refund came through. That complicates matters. And you also want to know not just how much profit you made, but how much risk you needed to take on to get there (that is, your volatility). So, there are quite a few ways to work out your return.

CAGR, or compound annual growth rate is a time-weighted average, calculated by taking your trading profit as a percentage of the average of your beginning of year capital (B) and end of year capital (E). The formula is *(E - B) x ([E + B] / 2)*. This is your trading return; you need to ensure it covers your office and other costs!

So, for instance, if you trade for a year on $100,000 starting capital and your trading capital is $125,000 at the end of the year, you'll want to calculate your trading return *($125,000 - $100,000)* = **$25,000** as a percentage of *([$100,000 + $125,000] / 2)* = **$112,500.**

So your CAGR is *$25,000 / $112,500 = 22.2%.*

Using your starting capital of $100,000 would have given you a return of *25%*, which is unrealistically high. That is $25,000 / $100,000 = 25%.

However, if you pay yourself a salary out of your account, that diminishes your trading pool. Or if you add capital once you feel more confident, that increases your trading pool. You'll need to find a way of making allowances for additions and withdrawals, or your performance won't be accurately shown. There are various ways of doing this.

The **Simple Dietz method** is the simplest way to do it. You simply adjust the beginning and ending amounts for cash inflows and outflows. The trading profit is shown *less* deposits and *plus* withdrawals, while your trading capital is shown *plus* deposits and *minus* withdrawals. It's really easy to calculate. However, it isn't particularly accurate, because it doesn't allow for the timing of cash flows.

So suppose you have the same figures as the CAGR example before, except that you took out $1,000 for a downpayment on a new car, and added $5,000 out of savings later on. Your trading profit is now shown as $25,000 *less* $5,000 deposit and *plus* $1,000 withdrawals = ***$21,000***.

You calculate this on your starting capital adjusted for changes. That is, $100,000, adjusted for *half* the inflows and outflows. Assuming, it happened half way through the year - though of course that might not be true!

In other words, *less* $1,000 withdrawn and *plus* $5,000 added gives us $4,000 net, and we take half of this which is *$2,000* to add to the starting capital of $100,000, giving us ***$102,000*** total capital.

The rate of return is *$21,000 / $102,000 = 20.5%*.

The **Modified Dietz Method** is more complicated and aims to solve the problem of just assuming that all your withdrawals and additions happen halfway through the year. Each cash flow event is multiplied by a time factor, so that your starting capital is adjusted by:

$$[(T - t) / T] \times (CF \times t)$$

Where T is the total time period (e.g. 12 months) and t is the time of the cash flow (e.g. 6, for June, 10 for October and so on). If, from this, you have got the idea that Modified Dietz is somewhat clunky to use, you would be right. However, Wikipedia conveniently supplies an Excel VBA file that you can use to automate the calculation.

To get an even more accurate idea you could use a **time-weighted rate of return.** You divide the year into different periods, with a new period beginning every time you increase or decrease your trading capital. You then calculate the CAGR for each individual time period, then those returns are multiplied to arrive at the CAGR for the year as a whole. It gives you a much more accurate idea of your profitability, but the math is complex. Fortunately, you can use apps and websites like **https://www.rateofreturnexpert.com/time-weighted-return-calculator** to do it for you automatically.

Another way of calculating returns is the **dollar-weighted rate of return**, but while it works for investors, it's not really useful for traders because it can't deal with large negative values. In the nature of things, traders quite often do have a negative return for a day, a week, or possibly a month or two - rarely, but occasionally even for a year.

What risk did you run to get this return?

You might think $100,000 is a lot of money. But if I asked you to play Russian roulette with a gun with five chambers loaded and one empty, you might think it's not a lot of money compared to the risk of losing your life. In trading, things are less extreme, but that's a vivid example of why you can't get useful information from looking at returns without considering the risks that you took on in order to get those returns.

The win/loss percentage is one way of assessing whether your risk level is appropriate. A stable percentage of winning trades is a good sign; a handful of big wins making up for long losing streaks is not. It's a good idea to use standard deviation to check on your performance. This will show how much your monthly or daily performance varies from your average. Almost all trading software will now do this automatically for you, but the steps are quite simple if you use a spreadsheet;

• find your *average* return over the period, let's say 10%,

• subtract the *average* from each daily return (so if you made 25% today, that would be *25% - 10% = 15%*. If you made 5% today, that would be *5% - 10% = minus 5%*, for instance),

• square the *differences* you found (this will cancel out and get rid of all the negative numbers, e.g. -5 x -5 = 25),

• add these numbers to get the *sum of the squares*,

• and finally, calculate the *square root* ($\sqrt{\ }$) of the sum of the squares, to get the *standard deviation*.

The sum of the squares will be higher, the more diverse your returns. If every day, day in, day out, you made a 10% return, then your difference every day would be zero and the squares would be zero, and the sum of the squares would be zero, and the standard deviation would be zero. This is, of course, never actually going to happen. If you are taking 11% some days and 9% others, your difference to your average 10% will only be 1, and 1 squared is 1, and the square root of one is one... However, more likely your differences on both sides will be more significant, and the larger they are, the larger your standard deviation.

A high standard deviation, that is, very widely varying daily or monthly performances, suggests you are taking on a relatively large amount of risk. A low standard deviation usually correlates to a less risky trading strategy. In fact, it's useful to know the standard deviation of a strategy you've backtested, because even if it works out, it might have a higher level of risk than you feel comfortable with.

This may sound quite theoretical, so let's just consider a very simple history of *five days* of trading by two traders. Both Albert and Barbara have an *average* return of 10%, but their day-to-day experience is a bit different.

Albert is incredibly steady, scoring daily returns of 10%, 12%, 8%, 9% and 11%.

Barbara has good and bad days - 20% up, 20% down, 25% up, 10% down, and finally pulling the iron out of the fire with an amazing 35% up return on the fifth day.

Remember, we are calculating the difference to their average return of 10%. So calculating the differences for Albert; 0 on day 1, when he makes exactly his average return of 10%; then +2 when he makes 12%, -2 when he makes 8%, -1 when he makes 9% and +1 when he makes 11%.

What about Barbara? When she makes 20%, take 10 from 20 and you get a difference of +10. The next day, she's *down* 20%, though, the difference between 10 and -20 is -30. Day after she's *up* 25%, take 10 from 25 and you get a difference of +15. Then she's *down* 10% the next day, so that's 10 and -10 which is a -20 difference. And finally, after the amazing fifth day, she's *up* 35%, so take the difference between 10 and 35, and you get +25.

Now, to get the squares, just multiply each number by itself (that is, each *difference* by itself) and then add them all together. This is where there's a really huge difference.

Albert: $(0x0 + 2x2 + 2x2 + 1x1 + 1x1) = (0 + 4 + 4 + 1 + 1) = \mathbf{10}$

Barbara: $(10x10 + 30x30 + 15x15 + 20x20 + 25x25) = (100 + 900 + 225 + 400 + 625) = \mathbf{2250}$

Albert gets a total of 10. Barbara gets a total of 2250!

The *square root* of 10 is 3.16, and that is the *standard deviation* of Albert's performance.

On the other hand, Barbara has a standard deviation of 47.43 (square root of 2250). You can probably have a guess at their different styles of trading from those figures.

Investors usually compare their performance with a relevant benchmark, such as the S&P 500. They want to know that they are getting returns that compare well with the market. However, there is no central benchmark of trading performance. You might look at how EToro's top traders are doing as EToro has a 'copy trader' program which lets you copy their trades. However, they are swing traders and investors for the most part, not day traders.

Having a winning market mentality

All good athletes will tell you that to get top performance, they need to use their heads as well as their muscles. Golfers will visualize their swing before they take it; marathon runners do less running in the last week before the race, but spend a lot of time thinking through the race, dividing it into smaller sections and setting their goals for those.

Traders are just the same. To trade really well, you don't just need stock quotes and scanners and screens and charts and a methodology, you need to have your head in the right place. You need to be cool enough that if there isn't a good trade you can see anywhere, you say, "Okay, it's not a good time to trade." A bad trader, on the other hand, will lower their expectations and take a trade that has a very poor risk/reward ratio just to feel that they've done *something*. Have the discipline to wait till the good trades appear.

Don't get careless. You may think it's crazy, but I still talk myself through my trades, or more accurately, mumble myself through my trades. It means that I have to have a proper game plan, with entry and exit points, stop-loss, and a quantified risk ratio. It also makes it much, much more difficult to lie to myself about the trade. (Bad traders do that a lot.)

I *never* calculate what I'm making on a trade, except when I calculate the risk/reward ratio right at the start. I might make $20 and I might make $200, but my focus is on getting the trade right and protecting my downside. Treat the market as if it's a horse and you're a horse whisperer - be patient and let it come to you. If you start thinking about the money, and cheering the share price on, you're getting emotionally involved - and you're going to start lying to yourself.

Don't beat yourself up if you make a losing trade or a mistake. Think it through rationally - is there something you could and should have done differently? Did you protect the downside? - and then just let it go and move on to the next trade.

Keep yourself grounded, and you'll be a much better trader. No greed, no fear, no brain fog or panic - if that's you, you're already ahead of 90% of other traders.

Chapter 9 Quiz

1. How do you know your strategy will work?
   a) It was recommended by a well-known, successful trader
   b) You backtested it thoroughly
   c) All the times you have seen this pattern, the trade was successful
   d) You can't

2. When should you not trade?
   a) When you are feeling panicky
   b) When you can't see a trade that fits your strategy
   c) When you are feeling angry about a losing trade
   d) When you are hung over

3. What does the standard deviation of your returns tell you?
   a) How much money you are making on each trade
   b) How much overall return you are making
   c) How much risk you are taking to make your return
   d) The average beta of the stocks you traded

4. Why might 'paper trading' or simulation not produce accurate results?
   a) Because your emotions aren't fully engaged
   b) Because it doesn't allow for currency exchange
   c) Because the software is unreliable
   d) Because your orders might not have been able to be filled in real life

5. Which of these is not a way of calculating your return over time?
   a) The Modified Dietz
   b) The Bourne Ultimatum
   c) Dollar weighted rate of return
   d) CAGR

10

Chapter 10: Good Traders Make Good Losses

Is there such a thing as 'good' losses? Yes, there is - a good loss is one that stops you from making a bigger loss. In other words, it's a loss that you defined before you made the trade, and that you controlled successfully.

A 'good' loss is also one that you learn from. You might learn that you're doing the right thing, that you entered and stopped the trade correctly and it was simply one of the times the odds weren't on your side. Or you might learn that you need to check confirmation, that a certain trade is becoming less profitable, or that you were too optimistic going into the trade.

In order to learn from your losses, you need to write down every time you win *or* lose a trade, what happened; why you entered the trade; what happened; what you will do next time. Write it down. Don't just think about it, write it down. That stops you forgetting what you've learned.

You're also going to write your trades down so that you can cut those bad trading emotions - over-confidence (when you win) and fear and panic (when you lose). Once the trade is written down, you've written it *out* of your mind. You can turn the page - quite literally.

What could you do differently next time? Sometimes, nothing. You entered a trade, everything was correct, unexpected news flipped the stock price and you got stopped out correctly with a small loss. You just need to accept that sometimes things don't work out.

Sometimes, the price goes through your stop-loss order and you can't manage to exit the stock at your stop-loss price. In this case, you really need to go for what you can get - even if it's a lower price. Otherwise, you're like the guy who, when his taxi driver drove off a cliff, asked, "At least stop the meter, can't you?"

Sometimes, you recognize that you got greedy. You hung on for a bit more after the stock hit your profit target, and then it fell back again. You get out, if you're lucky, with a small profit - more likely, after it's passed through your buy price and hit your stop-loss. So next time, the one thing you'll do that's different is that you will sell, or sell part of your position, or set a trailing stop-loss, when you hit the price target. Any of these actions would prevent you getting greedy and forgetting the basic reason why you're in the trade.

Another sign of greediness is buying into stocks that are going up real fast. That's particularly the case if they're being bid up by being tipped on a finance TV show or by chatroom or social media interest. It's always good to see a strong upward trend, but stocks that are going too fast, where the trendline is beginning to look more like a space rocket than a Boeing 747 taking off, are riding for a fall. What would you do differently next time?

Maybe, in this case, you bought on emotion, without taking the time to analyze the chart and set a target price and stop loss. Maybe you bottled out of taking your stop-loss, only to see the stock plunge even further. So next time, you quiet your emotions long enough to do proper analysis, and if you've got things wrong, you take your medicine and activate your stop-loss.

Did you get careless? Placing a market order and getting filled at a price that was too high to make a profit? Did you get distracted by a delivery or something on TV, and then the market went against you? Your losses are telling you that you need to smarten up your act. You need to concentrate more, and if you want to wander off and watch daytime TV, then at least close your positions first. Or maybe you worked out the position size wrong and took too much risk. Maybe you bought 1000 shares when you meant 100. It's been done before.

Good losses are small losses

How do you keep losses small? By risk management. By taking the right size of position and giving your trade a tight stop loss. By discipline. And by not taking it personally.

Be good at being wrong!

Trading is not like running in a race, when you have to come first or you lose. It's like playing baseball. You might hit a home run, you might get to first base. You might get one of your team home who is already on third base. The more you hit, the more your team scores. You just have to keep hitting. And there's no strike out in trading!

However, I will suggest that you might want to take time out if you have three losing trades in a row, or if you lose more than $1,500 (or whatever number makes sense in terms of your particular account value). Do this *mechanically* and make it into a trading rule, because so often we say to ourselves, "I am not angry! I am not emotional!" when actually, we're just a fiery little ball of rage after a couple of trades went bad. If you invoke the time out rule, you won't be able to lie to yourself, and you won't be able to lose any more money trying to make back what you've already lost.

Remind yourself that good traders can and do lose trades. If you ask successful traders their win/loss ratio, they'll often tell you, and it often will be quite moderate, like 60-70%. That means they're losing a third of the time or more. How can they be successful with that win rate? Because their profits make significantly more money than their losses lose.

This is why you need to learn to love a 'good' loss; one executed neatly and in line with your original trading plan, and that minimizes your risk level and the negative impact of a run of bad trades. Never, ever, double down. That's a viable plan for investors who can buy a stock when it's down and wait two or three years; maybe they're even getting paid good dividends while they wait. It is not a viable plan for traders - it increases your risk.

A loss taken is a risk avoided. I know the proverb is "Never *catch* a falling knife," but trying to hold on to a falling knife is equally painful.

And to finish this chapter, let's read a boxing quote which resonates with this chapter beautifully.

"Even the greatest all lost and came back. That's just part of it." Deontay Wilder after his loss to Tyson Fury in the world heavyweight championship bout.

Chapter 10 Quiz

1. What is a 'good' loss?
   a) One that is less than 2% of your portfolio
   b) One that you stop lossed out correctly
   c) One that doesn't bankrupt you
   d) One that is less than 10% of the risk taken

2. Which of these might lead to your losing money on a trade?
   a) Greed
   b) Over-confidence
   c) Carelessness
   d) Fear

3. How can you keep losses small?
   a) Manage your money correctly
   b) Use leverage
   c) Use stop losses with discipline
   d) Only trade small cap stocks

4. What can you learn from your losses?
   a) Whether you tend to be too optimistic
   b) Whether a certain type of trade is becoming less productive
   c) Whether you get distracted too often
   d) Whether Goldman Sachs is making money

5. Which of these is something you'd want to record about a losing trade?
   a) The price you bought at
   b) How you felt at the time
   c) Whether in retrospect you made an obvious mistake (e.g. not looking for confirmation before trading)
   d) What the market was doing at the time

11

Chapter 11: Strategies that Work

A strategy for getting started

Some people jump into trading. But it may be best, at first, to ease into trading, gently.

If, for the first couple of days, you just focus on watching a single stock, you can learn a lot about the market in a very concentrated way. You might just spend half an hour a day, till you are able to stay focused for that length of time, and then increase it - don't risk being zoned out because you're trying to concentrate for too long. Catch the open, stick around for half an hour, and you will start learning fast. Trading is a bit like meditation, it takes practice to keep your mind in the right place for more than a couple of minutes!

Track how your stock opens, whether there's a breakout or a reversal. Track the trading volumes. Extend your time till you can watch that stock all day, from the open to the close; what happens as the market comes up to the close and traders need to settle their positions?

Check how the stock trades against its sector index or against the market. Check how it trades against another leading stock in its sector, for instance Realty Income against WJ Carey, Apple against Microsoft, KO against PEP. (If you don't know that last pair of tickers, look them up.)

And at the same time as you're watching the stock on the screens, you want to be flicking between different time period charts, looking to see how it's been behaving over the last month, three months, the last year. Ascertain the trendlines and important support and resistance levels.

Write down, or voice record, everything you notice. The aim isn't to sit there passively, it's to get into the rhythm of the market and learn to spot signals that the share price is going to behave in a particular way. Once you're ready, just *think* about doing that first trade. Think through the set-up, or even better, talk yourself through it aloud; your target price, your stop-loss level, your total risk, and what will be the confirmation that you need to trade, for instance, a doji or a five-minute close above the resistance level.

And then you can trade if you want to, on paper or for real. No hurry. Because you have used this trade to talk through the process, without necessarily having to trade, you'll keep calm; no pressure. This is the way you want to feel every time you trade. Observe how the trade plays out, but don't get hung up on it. It's just one trade. I have done thousands.

Separately from this exercise, remember to do your practice on the keyboard. Practice those hotkeys and practice setting up orders. That will also help to de-stress real trading and ensure your fingers are as fast as your mind. Let's now look at a few tried and tested strategies for day trading successfully.

ABCD

This really is as easy as ABC!

The ABCD setup consists of four reversal points, making the chart pattern look like a slanted W or a bolt of lightning. It can work for long or short trades. I'll describe it for long trades since if you're starting out in day trading, your broker may not let you short a stock.

You're looking for a stock that has hit a significant high at A. Scanning for stocks hitting new highs will give you your basic watch list here.

You then watch as the stock falls to B.

It then bounces up to C, but not quite all the way back to A. This is where it meets resistance and falls again to D, which is a bit lower than B.

At D, you're looking to buy for another reversal.

An example is shown on the next page, but the perfect ABCD conforms to a number of criteria.

• It starts with a significant swing high or low (A to B).

• The countertrend (B to C) only partially retraces the first leg of the pattern. It's always the shortest leg in the pattern.

• The resumed trend leg (C to D) should be the same length as the first leg (A to B). This symmetry is important.

• In a downtrend, point C must be below point A (and in an uptrend point C must be above point A) - if the price falls all the way back to point A, you don't have an ABCD pattern.

• And finally, point D must be a new price high or low compared to B.

You then buy at D, looking for a bullish reversal. Look for confirmation from breached resistance levels, a bullish formation in the candlestick chart (e.g. a hammer doji).

Your stop loss should be set just below D, and your price target is C. Sometimes, with a strong overall bullish trend, the price may continue up, so lighten your position at C by taking out your initial investment, but run the rest of the position until you see a bearish signal or the price breaks to the downside of the bullish trendline.

The nice thing about ABCD is it can happen twice in the same stock on the same day. The second pattern will probably be a bit smaller, and on lower volume, but you can still make money out of it.

Gap and Go

To play Gap and Go, you need to scan for stocks that have gapped up strongly in pre-market trading. This strategy works really well on stocks in the $10-20 price range and that have relatively limited float. You need to see volume, and you need to check out that there's a fundamental reason behind the move, like an earnings release. The higher the volume and the faster the price movement, the better the opportunity.

Look how SCWorx Corp traded after gapping up, with very high volumes. Although it saw a pullback half way through the run, you would not have missed the boat even if you had bought in late, at $3. The stock ran all the way to $4 before it ran out of steam.

Get your orders ready, because timing is everything with this strategy. The first one-minute candlestick sets your price range. You'll need your charting frequency set at one minute for this trade and yes, you'd be right that I forgot that when I plugged in this chart. The top is your entry price, and the bottom is your stop. And in you jump!

If you miss your first chance at Gap and Go, wait for a pullback - to give you a second chance. If you're not an experienced trader, it will be a more relaxed trade than trying to hit the market open. Look at the pullback to just below $3 - if you had missed the first chance to buy in, this still gives you the entry to the Gap & Go trade.

There is also a slightly later third chance. You *might* have traded from those two green candlesticks just after 16:30, marking the end of a consolidation period, and running from $3.10 to $3.50 or so. But this is not such a great trade and I probably wouldn't have taken it, particularly because there was very little trading volume behind it.

Fallen angel

This is a variant on Gap and Go, and is another trade for market open. The fallen angel stock makes a new high in early trading, but then sells off quickly, on high volume (the trading volume is important for this trade).

Watch the stock. It might carry on downwards, in which case, leave it well alone. But if it consolidates, and holds a support level (such as the low of the pre-market, the 5-day moving average), keep watching until you get confirmation. Confirmation for your trade is high volume again combined with a new one-minute high. If you get the high but without the volume, don't bother with the trade.

Like Gap and Go, this strategy works for low-float stocks but probably won't work for big caps. There are too many high-frequency trading programs involved with the big caps and their computer algorithms will get there before you do. And even with low-float stocks, it is a trade that you should only use once you have some experience, because the drops can be quite fast, as well as the run-ups.

VWAP Trading

Institutional traders who are working for the big banks are often judged by the relationship of their trades to VWAP - the volume weighted average price. Since they have to trade very large blocks of stock, they often have to do so gradually. VWAP, being adjusted for volume, is a better benchmark for them than the unadjusted price index, in which a small trade might have been done for a better price. So the big institutional traders always look to buy or sell close to the VWAP - and that's interesting information for day traders, because it sets up a pattern that can be used to predict price actions.

If a stock tests the VWAP, then one of two situations is likely to happen.

1. Nothing much, because there is no big institution wanting to buy or sell in high volume.

2. A breakout, because a big trader is buying, or breakdown, because they have a line of stock they want to get rid of.

Obviously, you want to get situation 2, but the fact that the alternative is 'nothing much' limits your downside if the trade doesn't work out.

Suppose a stock moves up in early trading, then falls back, with good volume, I'm going to watch the VWAP. If the chart confirms that the stock has found support from the VWAP, then I will go long. A confirmation means it has to have touched the VWAP and bounced off it *twice*. You're looking for candlesticks standing with their tails on the VWAP. If nothing much happens, I can get out. If I get a breakout, I'm ahead.

Alternatively, VWAP might tell you to go short. If a stock has fallen, then moves up, but just hits the VWAP, finding resistance, going short will keep you in the continued downward trend.

So, in the chart below, you can see the stock flattens out at the top, and then suddenly falls very fast. It then seems to consolidate and even moves upwards a little, but it still doesn't manage to break through the VWAP (the red line) to the upside - in fact, it doesn't even get close. When it begins to fall again, as you can see from the line downwards of red candlesticks, you can go short for the continuation of the downturn.

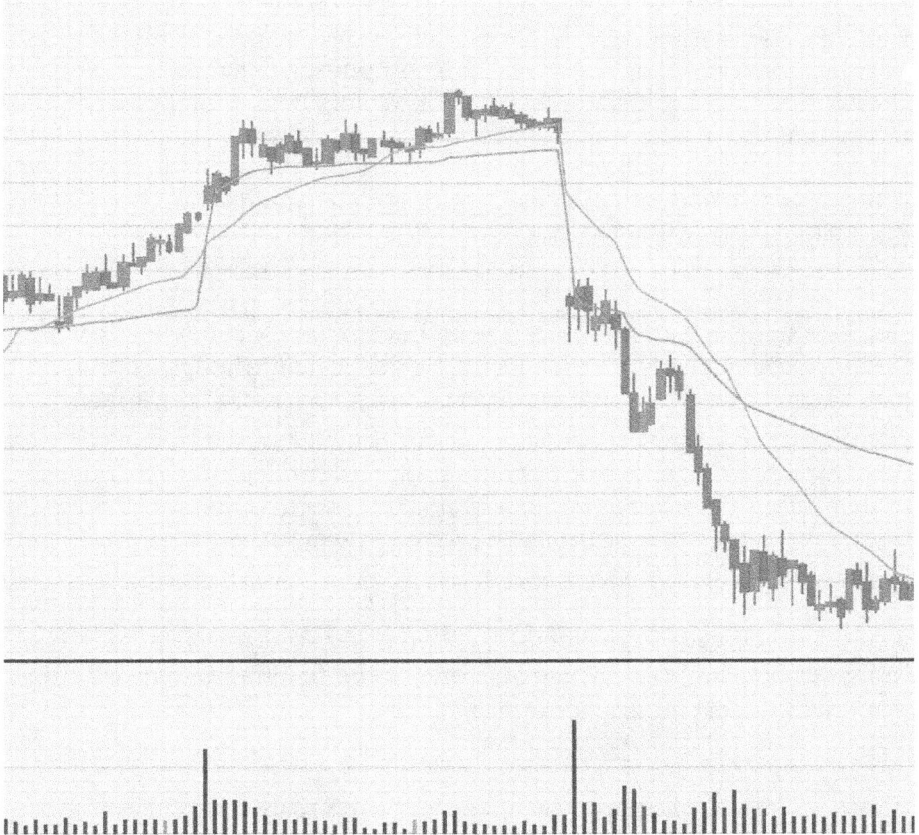

Trade the TRIN

You can run a stock chart with the TICK or TRIN indicator shown at the bottom of the chart. These indexes track rises against declines in stocks traded on NYSE and Nasdaq, respectively. Remember, the 'trading indicator' represents advances *divided* by declines, relative to advance volumes *divided* by decline volumes. If it's less than 1, the buyers are winning, and if it's above 1, the sellers are winning. Extreme levels are often an indication of a reversal. So, by putting your individual stock against the TRIN, you get a feeling of how it is performing compared to the market.

Alternatively, if your charting package doesn't let you do this, then just run the TRIN in a separate window.

The best trade is quite tricky to explain but easy to execute. First, you look for an extreme high in the TRIN, which often (though not always) indicates a fall in prices is likely. This then has to be confirmed by a pronounced fall in the stock price. Third, you look at the Bollinger Bands for your stock. If the stock price tests the lower edge of the bands *but it doesn't go through the band,* but instead it starts to rise again, go long on the stock at this point with a stop loss very slightly below the band.

Run this trade with large stocks like Apple and Amazon. It doesn't really work with smaller caps. In fact, it's one of the few trades that really does work with the big gorilla stocks.

Why does it work? Because you have identified a market in which advances are outnumbering declines, a bullish market, and an uptrend. With the fall in price you have identified a pullback within that uptrend. When the pullback doesn't break through the Bollinger Bands, you've found a good probability that the uptrend will continue.

ORB - Opening Range Breakout

Before the open, search for stocks that gapped up or down yesterday. This will bring out some investors who look at the movement and want to take a profit. For instance, a stock that was *up* 15% yesterday on good results might see plenty of holders wanting to sell at the open.

Wait out the first five minutes, and then pull up the five-minute candlestick. It may well be a very long 'pole' if the stock has traded up or down hard. Now, you simply wait for a candlestick to break out of the range represented by the *body* (not the wick or tail) of that candlestick. If it breaks downwards, enter a short trade; if it breaks upwards, buy the shares. Your profit target is the next key level, but you should also exit the trade if there is a new 5-minute low.

Alternatively, keep a watch on the opening trend, if it's all in bearish candlesticks, and wait till you see the first bullish candlestick.

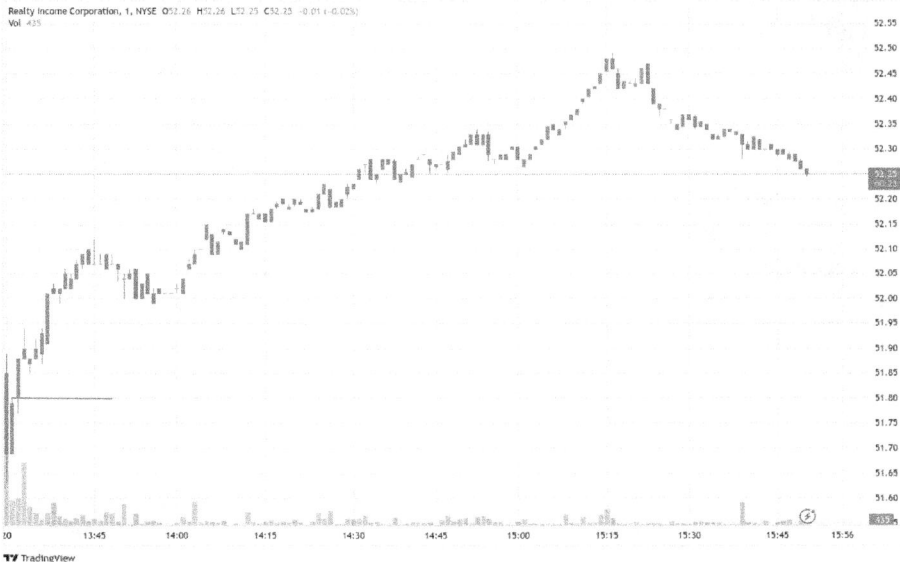

Doing your R&D

It's important that you keep refining your techniques. Markets change, and you may find that trades become less profitable over time, or that there's less liquidity in the markets you've been trading. Keep monitoring your results, and keep checking how you are doing.

You should also make time every month to do something to advance your knowledge. Buy a new book on advanced trading techniques, find some good YouTube videos to watch (there are some very bad ones out there, so be careful to get recommendations), or do some intensive work on charting techniques and technical indicators.

You can also analyze your previous trades to see what characterizes your best and worst trades, and where you make the most money. For instance, you may find that you're getting the best results from trading a particular type of setup, or during the first hour of trading. You might even find that all your afternoon trades are losing you money, or that you're making almost nothing on your bull flag trades but a whole load of money on head and shoulders patterns. A small fine-tuning can bring in a whole lot more profit.

You may also find that certain strategies play out best at different times of day. Gap-and-Go and Opening Range Breakout of course have to be played at the open, but trading with the trend tends to work better in the afternoon, for instance.

Chapter 11 Quiz

1. Why do you need to practise your keyboard skills?
   a) To enter trades accurately
   b) To enter trades quickly
   c) To de-stress the process of order placement
   d) So you can get a typist job if it all goes wrong

2. Which of these is not a trading strategy?
   a) Gap & Go
   b) Wash & Go
   c) VWAP trading
   d) Fallen angel

3. Which of these isn't something you need to track continuously?
   a) Support and resistance lines
   b) How a stock opens
   c) Trading volumes
   d) The interest rate

4. Gap & Go is a strategy that works
   a) At the market open
   b) At the market close
   c) Only when a company has results that day
   d) Only when a company had results yesterday

5. ORB stands for:
   a) One-off Reversal Breakout
   b) Opening Range Breakout
   c) Official Record of Bankruptcy
   d) Objective Range of Beta

12

Chapter 12: Top Tips for Each Aspect of Day Trading

The top rookie mistakes

1. Starting day trading without a defined and backtested trading strategy. That's gambling, and it's likely to fail.

2. Not writing a business plan and having detailed goals. Trading is a business and it needs to be treated as one.

3. Not having risk management systems such stop losses and daily close-outs, or not being disciplined enough to stick to them.

4. Betting the bank (and other poor cash management habits).

5. Trading too much. Make too many trades for too little profit, and you're making money for your broker, not for you.

6. Getting emotionally involved. The stock doesn't know that you own it, and a currency will not reward your loyalty or patriotism.

7. Letting trading take over your life. This will eventually wear you out.

8. Chasing the stock. Aim to buy when the stock is taking a rest, not when the share price is racing away.

The best ways to reduce your risk

1. Using and wherever possible automating tight stop losses.

2. Skim off the top of a position when the trade has reached your first price target.

3. Use a trailing stop loss, or increase your stop loss once your trade breaks even.

4. Limit the size of risk to 2% of your total risk capital.

5. Ensure all your positions are closed overnight.

6. Not trading when you are ill, tired, or have made a number of losing trades in succession.

Why day trading might not be right for you

1. You prefer to analyze companies to invest in and invest in them long term. If you really enjoy doing this, you probably will be bored day trading.

2. Self-discipline isn't your strong suit.

3. You enjoy gambling. If so, gamble with your pocket money, in a casino or at a racetrack. It's more fun and if you only gamble with cash, what you take with you is all you can lose.

4. You can't imagine spending all day on your own in front of computer screens. Day trading is not a good life for you if you want to see people or be in the great outdoors all day.

5. You're a very emotional person who uses gut feeling and instinct a lot of the time. That won't work in day trading.

6. You are good at putting things off until another day.

7. You want to get rich quick.

The top accessories that will make your trading station a pleasure to use

1. A really ergonomic chair that gives you proper support and is fully adjustable.

2. An adjustable standing desk so that you can stretch when you need to.

3. Excellent LED desk lamps with flexible or articulated arms.

4. Plenty of yellow legal pads for taking notes or jotting down ideas.

5. A good pen holder or mug so you don't spend half your day looking to see where you put your pen.

6. A basket or tray for collecting up all the things that clutter your desk - pens, erasers, staplers, sticky notes, and so on.

7. A coffee corner with a French press, aeropress or Espresso machine, that isn't anywhere it can spill onto your desk.

Chapter 12 Quiz

1. Which is these is a top rookie mistake?
   a) Not having risk management systems
   b) Not having a comfortable chair
   c) Using only one trading strategy
   d) Making relatively small profits

2. Which of these will not reduce your risk?
   a) Using tight stop losses
   b) Limiting your position size
   c) Closing all your positions at lunchtime
   d) Closing all your positions overnight

3. Which of these do you not need on your trading desk?
   a) Good adjustable lamps
   b) Lots of notepads
   c) A tray to keep the desk tidy
   d) A cat

4. Day trading is not right for you if:
   a) You are a loner
   b) You are a math whizz
   c) You are a gambler
   d) You are a procrastinator

5. How much trading is too much?
   a) Three trades a day
   b) Ten trades a day
   c) When your total returns are below 20%
   d) When your broker makes more money than you do

I would just like to mention before we go onto the final chapter on Incorporating Your Day Trading Business, if you are finding this book useful so far – it would mean everything to me if you could spare just a few seconds and write a brief review on Amazon on how this book is helping you so far.

13

Chapter 13: Incorporating Your Day Trading Business

Note: this chapter is written for US-based traders. While the basic principles will be similar in all jurisdictions, if you're based in the UK, Europe, Asia or Canada, or if you're a digital nomad, the details will be different. Ensure you know what rules apply where you are.

Regulation and what it means for you

Regulation can be a difficulty for day traders. For instance, American citizens living in Europe may find it difficult to open trading or even investing accounts, since the regulations applying to them are different from those applying to other nationalities.

I already mentioned the Pattern Day Trading rules, which means if you're trading stocks, you'll need $25,000 in your account. US investors are also barred from trading Contracts For Difference, which is a way UK and European investors can trade the price movement of a stock without actually buying the stock.

But you also need to take care to stay on the right side of tax regulations.

Taxes for day traders

We all hate paying taxes (though tax pays for a lot of things we regard as civilized life, such as education, healthcare, and decent roads). What's particularly annoying, though, is when you pay more tax than you needed to because you failed to plan ahead, or didn't check the tax treatment of a transaction before you made it. And tax law as it applies to day trading is complicated. It can be different depending on the type of asset you trade, for instance.

US tax law divides short term capital gains (on assets held for less than a year, which let's face it, means all your positions if you're a day trader) from long term capital gains (on assets which you have held for a year or more). However, there are a few interesting wrinkles for day traders as this can depend on what kind of assets you are trading!

In the US, regulated futures contracts, non-equity options, and foreign currency trades are taxed 60% as long-term capital gains and 40% as short-term capital gains (the 60/40 rule). This is great for day traders, as 60% of your profits on these assets are taxed at the lower long-term rate. By contrast, if you day trade *shares*, you'll pay the higher short-term rate on all your profits. Because Uncle Sam says so.

Tax is tricky as both long term and short term capital gains tax have different rates, but it's easy to give an example if we make some basic assumptions. Let's suppose, then, that our fortunate, wealthy traders pay tax at the highest rate because they make so much money, Mr 'Shares' Trader pays short term capital gains tax at his highest marginal rate of income tax, which is 37%.

But Miss 'Futures' Trader pays this 37% rate on only 40% of her gains. On the remaining 60%, she pays only 20% tax. So she pays a blended rate of just 26.8% compared to Mr Shares Trader's 37%. That's a huge saving.

Mr Shares Trader	100 taxed at 37%	**37.0**
Ms Futures Trader	40 taxed at 37% 60 taxed at 20% long term rate	14.8 + 12.0 **= 26.8**

However, trading the spot market in currencies doesn't automatically benefit from the 60/40 rule. You'll probably want to work with an accountant, as there are two choices; to report trading profits as short-term capital gains (Section 988), or to treat your spot trades as if they were futures contracts (Section 1256). However, you'll need to make a once and for all choice; it won't be easy to change it later. You'll need to think not just about your trading business, but about your other tax affairs; for instance, whether a certain treatment would put you into a higher tax category.

Stocks

For the IRS to tax your day trading in stocks as 'trading' then you will need to tick a number of boxes. You need to trade regularly and continuously, your activity needs to be 'substantial', and you will be profiting from intraday price moves, not price appreciation over the long term or dividend income. You need to fulfill *all* of these requirements, not just one or two.

• What does 'substantial' mean? If you're not trading around 1,500 trades a year, it's unlikely the IRS will think you're a professional trader.

• What does 'regular' and 'continuous' mean? If you're not trading most days in the year; if you are part-time as a trader, and have a day job, the IRS is unlikely to consider you a 'trader' for tax purposes.

• The IRS says that, "If the nature of your trading activities doesn't qualify as a business, you're considered an investor and not a trader."

• And finally, the IRS probably won't even consider giving you professional status in your first year of trading.

If you do qualify as a trader, you'll find there are significant advantages. You can take a number of deductions that investors can't; you'll be able to set many of your business costs against tax. As an investor, you would be very limited in your ability to do so.

You need to be careful, if you have an investment portfolio as well as a trading book, to separate the two. Your long-term investments will be treated one way and your trading business another (if you have 'trader' status). It might be best to use two different brokers, and keep two separate sets of accounts, so that it's absolutely clear not just to you, but also to the IRS if they ever want to audit you.

Given the complexity of tax regulations for traders, it may be well worth your while employing a tax adviser. Talking to other reputable traders can help you find an adviser who understands this particular business; accountants may also have their own experts, or work with specialist tax advisers. It's important to recognize that not every professional will understand the specific needs of day traders; a CPA (Certified Public Accountant) will know how to do tax and keep accounts, but may not understand day trading. Enrolled agents, on the other hand, specialize in tax preparation, but won't be able to help you with bookkeeping or advice on financing your business.

You might also, at some point, need a tax attorney. Generally, though, you'll only want to call on one if you are involved in litigation or a dispute with the IRS.

The wash-sale rule

The wash-sale rule is a real annoyance for non-professional day traders. It's intended to stop investors selling shares to make a tax loss, then buying them back the day after, but unfortunately, most day traders also get caught in the net.

The wash-sale rule says that if you have both a loss *and* profit for a particular stock in the same 61-day period (30 days before and 30 days after the sale), you cannot deduct the loss from your taxes. Instead, the loss is added to the cost basis of the stock, that is, to the price that the IRS says you bought the stock at. *Eventually*, the result will be similar, but it means if you're trading, say, Apple every single day, you'll not be able to write off your losses as you go. They'll just be added to the cost base of your next trade. This may make your trading profit for tax purposes larger than you would have expected as you will be carrying your losses over.

It's also important that you keep meticulous records, because you'll need to account for all your trades in a stock together if you trade it several times, or trade it regularly throughout the year.

The wash-sale rule also covers 'substantially similar' securities. That includes options on the stock, so you can't avoid the wash-sale rule by trading the stock and then trading the option. However, futures contracts are not covered by the wash sale rule.

If you qualify as a trader according to the IRS rules, you can elect to be 'marked-to-market', which has a number of advantages for you as you will see soon.

Mark-to-market

This is a form of accounting that only qualified 'traders' according to the IRS rules can use. You'll need professional assistance to fill in Form 3115, and you also need to submit the form with your prior year's tax return.

With mark-to-market, you do not have to track individual gains and losses. Instead, you pretend that you bought your *entire portfolio* at the start of the year and sold it at the end of the year, and the resulting profit is treated as income instead of capital gain. Because of this being treated as income on the entire portfolio, the wash sale rule no longer applies - you can buy and sell the same individual stock all day long, every day of the year.

Costs you can deduct

If you are day trading as a business, you can deduct a number of business costs. Legal and accounting fees can be expensed, and if you end up needing clerical help you can also expense that. Office expenses can also be deducted from your tax, though if you have a home office you can only expense its upkeep if it is used *exclusively* for your business. You can also write off a certain amount against computers and other equipment.

Any *advice* on trading can be expensed. This includes subscriptions to newsletters and research services, subscriptions to chatrooms, books bought for your education, advisory services, and trade coaching. However, you can't deduct the cost of attending seminars, conferences or training courses. Uncle Sam doesn't want you taking a holiday in Hawaii at his expense, even if there happens to be a trader conference going on.

If you incur interest because you're trading on margin, and your broker charges you, then you can expense it. However, you *can't* deduct commissions as a cost. They still reduce your tax, but what you need to do is to add the commissions to the cost of the shares when you are working out your capital gain on a trade. The same is true for transfer taxes, should you pay any.

Using an IRA

You might consider sheltering your trading portfolio inside an Individual Retirement Account (IRA). You'll pay no taxes on any capital gains within the IRA. However, there are a number of limits. You can contribute only $5,000 a year to the account, though if you have a 401k from an employer you have left, you can roll that into the IRA.

However, your broker may limit your trading options. And you won't be able to withdraw any money till you are 59 1/2, unless you pay a 10 percent tax penalty. It's also worth thinking about how you will support yourself in retirement if you do manage to make losses in your IRA. If I was going to use my IRA I think I'd want to have a few years' successful trading behind me. Otherwise, use your IRA for long term investments and day trade a regular trading account.

Chapter 13 Quiz

1. How much do you need in your account according to Pattern Day Trading rules?
   a) $2,500
   b) $250,000
   c) $25,000
   d) $500

2. Which of these assets does not benefit from the 60/40 tax rule?
   a) Foreign currency trades
   b) Stock trades
   c) Regulated futures contracts
   d) Non-equity options contracts

3. Which of these is not a tax-deductible cost for a trading business?
   a) Subscription to a newsletter
   b) Accounting fees
   c) A trading seminar
   d) Books about trading and market

4. When does the wash-sale rule apply?
   a) If you make both a profit and a loss in the same stock in a 61 day period
   b) If you hold a stock for less than a year
   c) If you buy a stock and sell it within 30 days
   d) If you buy a stock and sell it the same day

5. Which of these doesn't count as R&D for a day trader?
   a) Reading this book
   b) Back-testing a trading strategy
   c) Watching a YouTube video on day trading
   d) Changing broker

Leave a 1-Click Review!

I would be incredible thankful if you could take just 60 seconds to write a brief review on Amazon, even if it's just a few sentences!

Customer reviews

⭐⭐⭐⭐⭐ 5 out of 5

4 global ratings

5 star		100%
4 star		0%
3 star		0%
2 star		0%
1 star		0%

˅ How are ratings calculated?

Amazon.com readers

http://www.amazon.com/review/
create-review?&asin=B0D9YM5CWY

Amazon.co.uk readers

http://www.amazon.co.uk/review/
create-review?&asin=B0D9YM5CWY

Conclusion

Now that you've read this book, I'd like to tell you that you're ready to trade; but that would be a lie. You are ready to take the next steps towards successful day trading, though; defining, back-testing and paper-trading your chosen trading strategy.

This means that by the time you actually put your money into a trade, you can be confident that you have a trading strategy that will make you money. Very, very few day traders start with that confidence. They cut corners, or trade on gut feel rather than solid strategies.

In this book, you've learned the basics about how markets work. The practicalities of trading, and the different kinds of financial assets that you might decide to trade have been briefly covered, together with the advantages and disadvantages of each market.

You've learned to identify some basic market patterns that have a high probability of working out in particular ways, giving you the opportunity to make trades with a known risk/reward ratio. You've learned how to put your orders through, and in particular, how to create a package of orders that can automate your trade.

You've read about the basics of technical analysis, including candlestick charts, and you've also read up on some strategies for day trading that you can start to employ. This is only an introduction to the basics; there's still a lot more you can learn, whether you decide to follow podcasts or YouTube traders, buy specialized books on technical analysis and particular trades, or find a mentor in the trading community.

I've also shown you how to limit your risks. Risk management is the bit of day trading that isn't fun and doesn't get talked about a lot, but it's absolutely crucial to making money reliably in the long term. Money management, tight stop-losses, and not betting the bank are the only way you can stay in the game without risking a run of loss-making trades forcing you to quit.

You've also looked at issues about human emotions such as fear and greed, panic, and even boredom in relation to trading. You also have a shopping list for your trading business, including software, hardware, and a few creature comforts.

I hope you now have a good idea of whether day trading is for you, and what the biggest challenges will be for you personally. Even if you've decided that day trading probably isn't a great career for you and you'd prefer to focus on another way to make money, at least I've managed to save you a huge amount of work and the possibility of losing your risk capital.

If you've decided day trading is what you want to do, then don't forget to choose your strategy, backtest it, practice trading in simulation, and get yourself well prepared before you actually make that first trade. You will be surprised, if you do your preparation properly, how easy and stress-free day trading can be.

On the other hand, of course, you could just rush off and put all your money into a fast-rising stock you heard about on TikTok. But I don't recommend it.

May all your trades be good ones!

HOW TO GET THE MOST
OUT OF THIS BOOK

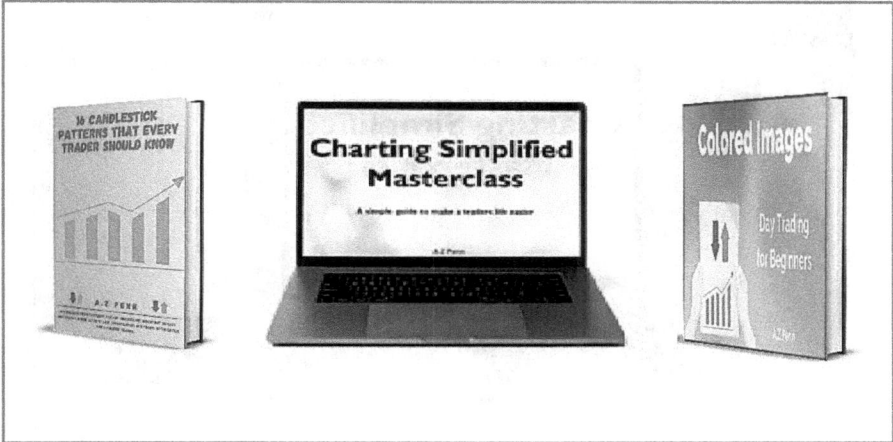

To help you along your trading journey, I've created a free bonus companion masterclass which includes video analysis of real life stock examples to expand on some of the key topics discussed in this book. I also provide additional resources that will help you get the best possible result.

I highly recommend you sign up now to get the most out of this book. You can do that by going to the link or scanning the QR code below:

www.az-penn.com

Free bonus #1: Charting Simplified Masterclass ($67 value)

In this 5 part video masterclass you'll be discovering various simple and easy to use strategies on making profitable trades. By showing you real life stock examples of a few charting indicators - you will be able to determine whether a stock is worth trading or not.

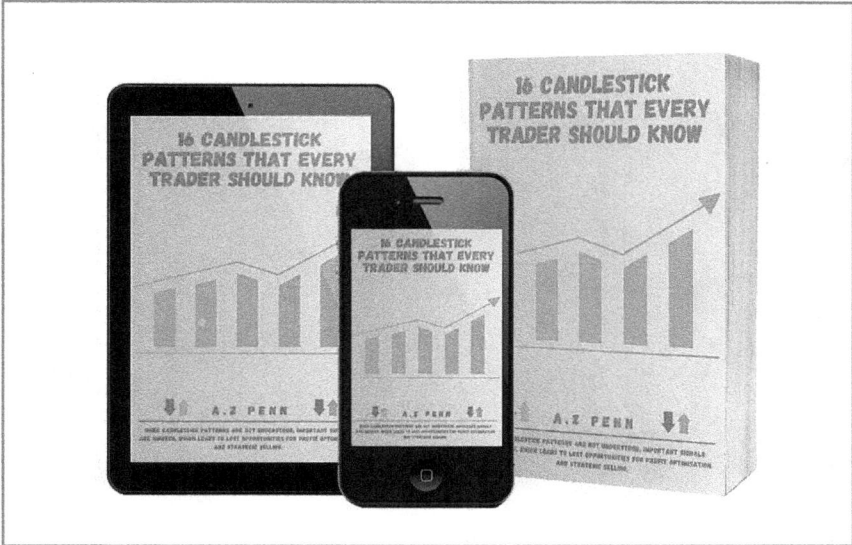

Free bonus #2: **16 Candlestick Patterns that Every Trader Should Know ($17 value)**

Stay ahead in the trading game with our essential guide on the patterns that are vital for reading market signals, identifying trend reversals, and making profitable trades. Equip yourself with the knowledge to make informed decisions and maximize your trading returns.

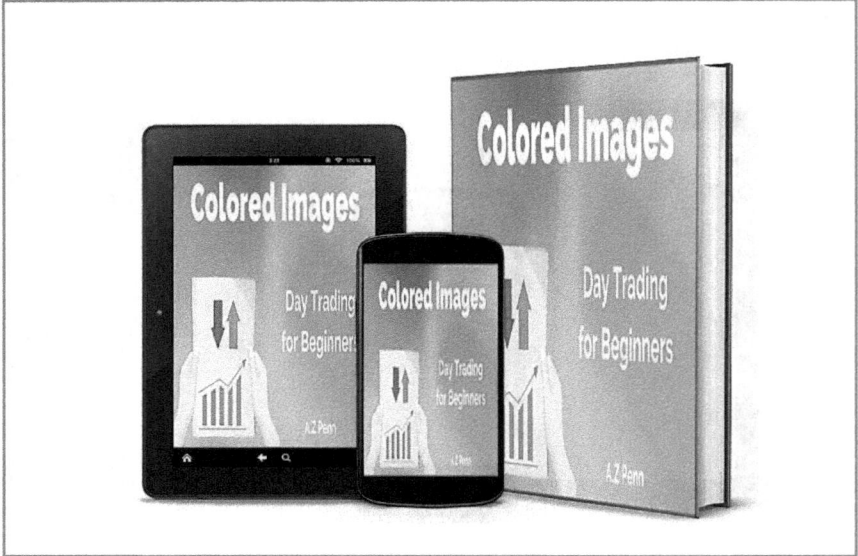

Free bonus #3: Colored Images – Day Trading for Beginners

To keep our books at a reasonable price for you, we print in black & white. But here are all the images in full color.

All of these bonuses are 100% free, with no strings attached. You don't need to provide any personal details except your email address.

To get your bonuses, go to the link or QR code:

www.az-penn.com

Glossary

Arbitrage - exploiting a difference in price for the same asset between two different markets. It's risk-free, but no longer very profitable for retail traders.

Ask price - the price at which you will be able to buy shares (the market maker 'asks' for this amount of money).

Basis Point - one hundredth of a percentage point: 0.01%.

Bear - someone who believes an asset's price is going down, and is selling the asset.

Bull - someone who believes an asset's price is going up, and is buying the asset.

Bull/Bear market - a rising and optimistic market / a falling, pessimistic market.

Bid price - the price at which you will be able to sell your shares.

Breakdown - share price movement down through a support level.

Breakout - share price movement up through a resistance level.

Call option - an option giving you the ability to buy shares at a particular date and price.

Channel - the space between the top and bottom trendlines.

Derivative - a security based on an underlying asset whose price movement is reflected in the derivative.

Divergence - when a technical indicator such as MACD or RSI does not move in line with the price of an asset.

Double bottom - a chart pattern of two successive and equal lows, suggesting a rebound could occur.

Double top - the reverse of a double bottom.

ECN (e.g. ARCA, Bloomberg, Instinet) - an Electronic Communications Network which links buyers and sellers directly.

EMA - Exponentially smoothed Moving Average, which gives more weight to the most recent price movements.

ETF - Exchange Traded Fund: a stock-exchange traded security that reflects the returns of a share index, commodity or other financial asset.

Expiration date - the date on which a futures contract expires.

Fill - the price at which your buy or sell order is executed.

Float - the amount of shares that actually trades, excluding shares held by insiders.

Futures contract - an agreement to buy or sell a standardized quantity of a commodity or currency at a specified future date.

Gap - a price move that is sudden enough to leave a 'gap' in the price chart.

Head and shoulders - a chart formation showing three consecutive highs, of which the second is the highest. Usually foreshadows a reversal of a bull trend and a fall in the share price.

Hedge - a strategy used to limit losses on a financial or real asset by using an opposing derivative or other trade, for instance, limiting the losses on a holding of shares by buying a put option which will make an offsetting profit if the share price goes down.

In-the-money - a call option (option to buy) is in the money when the strike price is less than the current share price.

Leverage - multiplying the return on an asset by using debt (buying on margin), or by using a leveraged derivative such as an option.

Limit order - an order that states the maximum price at which you will buy or the minimum price at which you will sell.

Liquidity - the ease with which an asset can be bought or sold. For instance, your home is not a liquid asset; shares in IBM are. Different shares and other securities have differing liquidity.

Long - to be long is to own an asset. A long position means you have bought the asset.

MA - moving average: an average of a number of time periods' prices.

Margin - the amount by which a broker will allow your trades to exceed the cash in your account. Effectively, you are borrowing from your broker.

Margin call - if the value of your assets falls below a specified amount, and you are trading on margin, a broker can ask you to deposit further funds to support your position. This is a margin call.

Market capitalization - the number of shares outstanding in a company multiplied by its share price.

Market maker - a broker/dealer who makes a market in a stock, offering both to buy and sell the stock from market participants.

Market order - an order to buy or sell an asset at the best price your dealer can get.

Momentum - the speed of price change. Momentum trading aims to 'go with the flow,' purchasing assets that are moving in an uptrend.

Odd lot - a lot of less than 100 shares.

Offer - the price at which you can buy a share: also known as the ask price.

Pip - in currency trading, the smallest amount that a currency can move: the fourth (last) decimal point.

Point - the minimum movement in the price of futures.

Put option - an option giving you the right to sell a share at a given price.

Rally - when having hit a low point, a share price begins to go back up.

Resistance - a price level which acts as a ceiling, creating an obstacle to further increases in price. Once passed, it becomes a support.

Retracement - after a strong run, a share will often retrace part of that move before continuing the trend.

Reversal pattern - chart patterns that predict a given trend will likely reverse. These include double and triple tops, head and shoulders, hammer and shooting star candlesticks.

Risk/reward ratio - measuring your potential loss against the potential profit of a given trade.

Round lot - 100 shares or a multiple of 100 shares.

Short - to sell an asset without having bought it, aiming to buy it at a lower price thus making a profit.

Short Sale Restriction - short sales at the bid price may be restricted if a share's price has fallen 10% or more during the current or previous trading session.

Spread - the difference between the bid and ask price - the prices at which you can sell or buy the shares.

Stock index futures - futures contracts taken out on a stock index such as the S&P 500.

Stop-loss - the price at which your trading strategy dictates you will close a loss-making trade.

Strike price - the price at which you can exercise an option to buy or sell the underlying shares.

Support - a significant price level which acts as a 'floor' to the price.

Swing trading - short-term trading in which market positions are not closed overnight.

Technical Analysis - analyzing share price charts in order to predict the likely course of prices.

Thin market - a market that has a low volume of trade.

Tick - a minimum movement of the share price upwards or downwards.

TICK index - subtracts the number of NYSE stocks currently ticking down from those ticking up - a good indicator of market sentiment.

Ticker symbol - the sequence of letters that identifies a security, e.g. AAPL for Apple, T for AT&T, or GRRR for Gorilla Technology Group.

Trailing stop - a stop loss that is ratcheted upwards as the share price rises, in order to protect profits.

Trend - a price pattern that shows a strong tendency in one direction.

Trendline - a line drawn linking the lowest lows or highest highs of a price chart, in order to show the trend.

TRIN - the Nasdaq equivalent of the TICK index.

VWAP - Volume Weighted Average Price, a moving average that is adjusted for the volume of trade.

Volatility - the amount by which an asset's price fluctuates around the average price.

Volume - trading volume, the number of shares bought and sold during a given time period.

Reference

Ardt, W. (2020). Risk and Money Management for Day and Swing Trading. Torero Traders School.

Aziz, A. (2016). How to Day Trade For a Living. Createspace.

Aziz, A. (2018). Advanced Techniques in Day Trading. Createspace.

Aziz, A & Baehr, M. (2020). Mastering Trading Psychology. Peak Capital Trading.

Cameron, R. (2015). How to Day Trade. AuthorHouse.

Holland, A. (2024). Day Trading Options: Strategies and Techniques for Profiting from Short Term Options Trading. Self-published.

Logue, A. C. (2014). Day Trading for Dummies. John Wiley & Sons.

Noonan, T. (2019). Day Trading QuickStart Guide. ClydeBank Finance.

Quinn, W & Turner, J. D. (2020). Boom and Bust: A Global History of Financial Bubbles. Cambridge University Press.

Tandler, J. (2012). The Mental Edge in Trading: Adapt Your Personality Traits and Control Your Emotions to Make Smarter Investments. McGraw Hill.

Turner, T. (2008). A Beginner's Guide to Day Trading Online. Simon & Schuster.

Quiz Answers

Chapter 1:
1. C
2. A
3. B
4. D
5. A

Chapter 2:
1. B
2. C
3. C
4. D
5. A

Chapter 3:
1. A
2. C
3. D
4. C
5. A

Chapter 4:
1. C
2. C
3. D
4. D
5. C

Chapter 5:
1. B
2. D
3. B
4. C
5. C

Chapter 6:
1. B
2. A, B, C
3. A
4. C
5. A

Chapter 7:
1. D
2. B
3. D
4. C
5. A, B, C, D

Chapter 8:
1. A
2. D
3. A
4. B
5. D

Chapter 9:
1. B
2. A, B, C, D
3. C
4. D
5. B

Chapter 10:
1. B
2. A, B, C, D
3. A, C
4. A, B, C
5. A, B, C, D

Chapter 11:
1. A, B, C
2. B
3. D
4. A
5. B

Chapter 12:
1. A
2. C
3. D
4. C, D
5. D

Chapter 13:
1. C
2. B
3. C
4. A
5. D

www.ingramcontent.com/pod-product-compliance
Lightning Source LLC
Chambersburg PA
CBHW071549210326
41597CB00019B/3176